Anger Management for a Zen Mind

MASTER YOUR EMOTIONS, CONTROL YOUR ANGER, AND SOOTHE THE FIRE WITHIN

Robert Hall

Table of Contents

Introduction

Don't worry, be happy. Words to live by. But honestly, an infuriating sentiment when you actually stop to think about it. Of course, in an ideal world we would love to be happy and not have to worry, or feel sad, or get angry. However, as we all know, the world is far from ideal. Even if it were ideal, it is doubtful that we, as human beings, could remain in a continuously happy state. Whether we like it or not, our brains are hardwired to feel a myriad of emotions. Emotions such as happiness, yes, but also emotions such as envy, humiliation, disgust, confusion, passion, compassion, grief, fear, loathing. Anger. Fury.

The human mind is a complex machine. It is programmed to think and feel not just in black and white but in a full spectrum of colors.

The human capacity to experience a range of complex emotions can be our greatest asset. Emotions can help us survive. Indeed, Charles Darwin believed that the emotion of fear is vital to the survival of a species, as it tells the animal when to flee from a threat.

Emotions can help us make decisions and motivate us to take action. When we are experiencing typically negative emotions such as sadness or anxiety, we are motivated to take steps to ensure that these negative feelings cease, often resulting in a better situation for ourselves and the people around us.

Perhaps most importantly for humans, emotions help us understand other people and help people better understand us. Emotional cues such as body language and facial expressions play a huge part in communication and allow people to build stronger and more meaningful relationships with others. Emotions could be considered the glue that holds together the fabric of society.

Certainly emotions can be seen as a huge asset to the human race and to the individual. However, if we are unable to control our emotions, it is possible for this asset to become an even greater liability.

Growing up, my brother and I played tennis. That was our sport. To be honest, I never really enjoyed the sport as a young boy. I never really had a talent for it. I played it because my older brother did and I guess my parents didn't want to have to drive to two different places every Saturday.

I remember we used to have competitions within our tennis club every now and then. Members of the club, the kids that we took tennis class with, would play against each other in mini tournaments. I would usually be eliminated from these competitions early because I stank. After being eliminated I would spend the rest of the Saturday watching my brother's matches. He would get quite far, often even making it into the finals. Aside from being a great tennis player, my brother was fiercely competitive. He always wanted to win and it was this desire that drove him to giving that little bit extra in every match. However, this desire to win also drove him to huge fits of anger when things didn't go his way.

Yes, my brother was a miniature John McEnroe when he played tennis. While he was too little to break his tennis racket, he would throw it around if he missed an important shot. While he never swore at the umpire, he would burst into hot, angry tears if a call didn't go his way. His tantrums got so bad that my parents eventually decided to pull both of us out of tennis. Not only was his behaviour upsetting to the other kids and parents, but it was also upsetting for my parents. My brother loved playing tennis but when he lost, he became inconsolable. It broke my parents' hearts seeing him like that.

It wasn't my brother's fault. He was just a kid. He hadn't developed the emotional intelligence to manage his anger, so when he played tennis, he played it with entirely unfiltered emotion. His emotions in this case were a double-edged sword. His passion for the sport and his desire to win made him a better player; much better than I, who didn't give a hoot about the sport. His anger helped motivate him to improve at the sport. Wherever he'd suffer a loss, he'd become mad at his own failings and this made him train harder in order to not lose again.

However, his uncontrolled anger soon revealed itself to be a weakness. When he started raging during a match, his performance dipped. His anger would make him act rashly, perhaps rushing the net for the quick point, when playing the baseline would've been the smarter play. When he lost a point, instead of analyzing his play-style and changing his strategy, his anger would cause him to blame others, such as the umpire or his tennis racket. If he felt a match slipping from his grasp, his resultant fury would exhibit itself in negative behavior, which had a negative impact on those around him. This damaged his relationships within the club and eventually cost him a beloved hobby.

My brother picked up tennis again eventually, once he was old enough to play with a more level head. He plays it to this day and enjoys it still. He still gets angry sometimes, but he is able to keep his anger under control and make it work *for* him instead of *against* him.

Anger is triggered by a combination of pain (either physical or emotional) and rage-triggering thoughts. "Thoughts that can trigger anger include personal assessments, assumptions, evaluations, or interpretations of situations that make peopleMills think that someone else is attempting (consciously or not) to hurt them" (Mills, n.d.). In my brother's case, the thoughts leading to his anger might have been that he thought that he wasn't good enough to win. It might've been that he thought the umpire was out to get him. It might have been that he thought he was letting down his family by not winning. It is likely that all of these thoughts were swimming in his mind at once, causing him pain on an emotional level. This combination of pain and negative thoughts would build up in his young mind as he played, eventually culminating in the spectacular outbursts of anger that I have previously mentioned.

Of course, my brother didn't want to be angry. It wasn't something that he consciously decided on. We are rarely in a position where we can decide how we feel about a situation. Emotions are generally automatic and instinctive. Anger, much like fear, is a natural and instinctive response to threats. It instigates aggressive behavior and drives us to defend ourselves when we are attacked; a basic instinct that allowed our more animalistic ancestors to survive the dangers of the past, ensuring the survival of the human race to this day. However, in modern society we cannot just go around attacking things that make us angry. We need to abide by social norms, laws, and common sense no matter how angry we may get. For this reason, it's important to understand that anger, as instinctive as it may be, is never uncontrollable.

Although anger, like all emotions, is a natural and important thing to feel, understanding our anger, managing it, and expressing it in the right way is equally important. By reading this book, you will gain a better understanding of your anger. Then you will be given the tools to manage your anger and express it in a healthy and productive way. Anger can be a great ally and motivator, but only if you can control the flames so that they don't burn you from the inside.

Chapter 1: Emotional Intelligence

Most people have heard of IQ, or intelligence quotient. You may have taken an IQ test in the past, most likely during school. IQ is a measure of a person's reasoning ability and is supposed to gauge how well someone can use information and logic to answer questions or make predictions. It is a concept that has been around for over a century and has been often used to determine whether a student is gifted enough to benefit from a more accelerated learning program. In the past, it has even been used to determine whether a candidate is suitably intelligent for a particular position in a university or company.

While IQ is a concept familiar to most people, you may not be as familiar with its younger brother, EQ, otherwise known as emotional quotient or emotional intelligence. If IQ is a measure of a person's logical reasoning ability, EQ can be described as a person's emotional reasoning. It is a person's ability to understand other people and how they may feel in any given situation. EQ enables you to better understand people's motivation and allows you to cooperate with them more effectively.

Needless to say, EQ is as important, if not more important, to success in today's world as IQ. As a society, most of us need to interact with several people during the course of our day-to-day lives, whether it be at work, at home, at school, or in social situations. Zhaoyang, R. (2018) states that the average person experiences 12 social interactions per day. That's 12 times we've had to speak with someone, understand how they're feeling (on a conscious or subconscious level) and interact with them without putting our foot in our mouth. The higher our EQ, the more successful our social interactions will be. Successful social interactions not only lead to healthier relationships with the people around us, but they can also lead to opportunities for advancements in our careers. Our managers tend to look on us more favorably if they enjoy talking with us and job interviews tend to be easier if we can understand the motivation behind each question. Emotional intelligence also leads to more successful negotiations as it allows both parties to utilize empathy to come to a mutual understanding and arrive at a mutually beneficial outcome.

Studies show that a high EQ can boost career success, leadership talent, entrepreneurial potential, relationship satisfaction, health, humor, and happiness. Understanding your emotions as well as the emotions of those around you is a key component to a successful and fulfilling life.

But can EQ be developed, or is it a measure that becomes set as we reach adulthood? The truth is, our inherent ability to manage our own and others' emotions is fairly stable and is influenced by early childhood experiences and even genetics. However, long-term improvements can be made even once we reach adulthood. It just takes dedication.

In order to explain why we should always be striving to improve our EQ and how we can seek to do so, let's take a more in-depth look at how emotional intelligence is measured.

THE FIVE CATEGORIES OF EQ

According to Akers & Porter, researchers in the field of emotional intelligence recognize five major categories. Each category is taken into account in the measurement of a person's EQ and each category plays an important role in daily life.

SELF-AWARENESS

Self-awareness is the ability to recognize an emotion as it happens. When talking specifically about anger, it is the ability to understand that you are feeling angry. With the benefit of hindsight, anger might seem like an easy emotion to recognize, but when you are caught up in the moment it is not always easy to take the time to recognize the emotion you are feeling. You may be so caught up in the situation that is triggering your anger that you just act without thinking. The emotion may come on so quickly that you don't have time to register it. Or you may be so accustomed to feeling angry that you dismiss the emotion as a state of normality.

Self-awareness requires having the emotional awareness to recognize your own emotions and their effects combined with an understanding of your capabilities and self-worth.

SELF-REGULATION

Self-regulation dictates the amount of time you allow yourself to experience an emotion. Although you can't dictate when you feel anger, once you are able to recognize you are feeling angry, you can dictate how long the emotion will last. This can be achieved by using anger management techniques such as taking a long walk, meditation, or casting the anger-triggering situation in a more positive light.

Self-regulation involves controlling your own disruptive impulses, being honest with yourself and others, adapting flexibility to changes, taking responsibility for your own actions, and being open to new ideas.

MOTIVATION

The ability to motivate yourself to achieve desired results is important but can be difficult to maintain. Difficulty arises when negative emotions or thoughts prevent you from seeing the point in the effort, or make a challenge seem insurmountable. However, if you are able to recognize negative thoughts as they occur and reframe them in a more positive light, this will help you maintain motivation. Motivation will require you to constantly strive for self-improvement, commit to goals, take initiative, and be optimistic.

EMPATHY

This is the ability to recognize how other people are feeling. It is the ability to place yourself in the shoes of someone other than yourself and understand their point of view. Not just this, but it is the willingness to take a step back from your own emotions and take the time to consider how the other person may feel. This combination of desire to understand and understanding can be very difficult, particular if you are predisposed to anger. When you are feeling angry, it may be so strong that you have a hard time thinking about your own emotional state, let alone that of the person that may be the cause of your anger.

As difficult as it may be, it is incredibly important to the maintenance of positive relationships and once you have mastered it, you will excel at things like anticipating the needs of others, developing and teaching others, reading the room, and communication.

SOCIAL SKILLS

Developing your social skills is hugely important to your success in life, both professionally and personally. Social interactions occur frequently in daily life and thus make up a huge part of our lives. Being adept in interacting with people will allow you to experience a range of benefits including being more persuasive, communicating your needs clearly, inspiring people, managing conflicts, collaborating with people, and building stronger bonds with people. While you may have a clear understanding of social etiquette and how you *should* behave in front of people, anger and other negative emotions can cloud your judgment, causing you to act in a way that goes against your rational understanding of acceptable standards of social behavior. Having a high EQ will help you understand your emotions, empathize with those around you, and communicate in a way that is not destructive.

EQ'S ROLE IN CONTROLLING ANGER

We've discussed how EQ is measured and its importance in life, but what is its role in controlling anger? How does having a high EQ translate to feeling less angry? Well, first of all, a high EQ in and of itself is not going to make you feel less angry. Nor should it, necessarily. It's important to remember that feeling anger is perfectly normal. The goal is not to feel less of it, but to recognize when you are feeling it, understand the impact it is having on you and those around you, and acting on it in a healthy manner. This is where EQ comes in.

UNDERSTANDING YOUR EMOTIONS

The first category of EQ is self-awareness. This involves recognizing when you are feeling an emotion, in this case, anger. Being able to recognize when you are feeling angry is the first step to being able to do something about it. The next step should be to understand *why* you are feeling angry.

We have previously discussed anger as an emotional response to pain, but it's not the only possible emotion to be born of pain. For example, let's talk about the emotional pain we suffer from the loss of a loved one. Depending on the individual, this pain can exhibit itself in emotions such as anger, yes, but also a whole host of other emotions including sadness, disbelief, loneliness, and guilt. It's possible for an individual to experience all of these emotions and more when dealing with this kind of pain. So, given all the possible emotions that one could experience in this type of situation, why do some people seem to predominantly feel anger?

Anger can often be a substitute emotion. This means that sometimes people choose to feel angry (either consciously or unconsciously) as a substitute to feeling pain. Rather than dwelling on the pain, some people distract themselves with anger and thoughts of righting the wrongs that have been inflicted on them. Rather than directing their thoughts within and confronting the pain that is inside them, anger enables people to direct their thoughts outwards. Rather than feeling vulnerable or frightened, they allow themselves to focus on how to get back at those that have wronged them.

This also allows people to feel powerful instead of vulnerable. It allows people to feel a sense of righteousness and makes the goal of punishing those that have wronged them feel entirely justified. Angry people always feel that their anger is justified and this sense of righteousness can be a powerful boost to one's self-esteem. When faced with a decision to feel this or feel the pain within, it is difficult not to choose the former.

However, problems arise when other people, the people around you and the people affected by your anger, do not agree that your anger, and the actions you have taken based on your anger, are justified. If a drunk driver accidentally takes the life of someone you love, you might feel angry enough to think that taking their life in vengeance is entirely justified. However, a judge and jury may disagree and you may go to jail for this kind of action.

This is an extreme example, but I'm sure you have found yourself in a situation where you have felt so angry that you wanted to punish the person that you felt had wronged you. It's okay. We have all had these thoughts. What's important is that we use our emotional intelligence to recognize our anger, understand that we are feeling anger because of pain, and objectively think of the best way to process this pain. "Anger cannot make pain disappear—it only distracts you from it" (Mills, n.d.). A resolution to your pain will rarely be found by getting angry and letting anger control you can often create more problems, which in turn lead to further pain, not just for yourself but for those around you.

EXERCISE EMPATHY

The fourth category of EQ is empathy; understanding the emotions of others. This is another key factor in your ability to control your anger.

Consider the following situation: you are behind on a deadline at work because you have been going through some personal issues. You ask your boss for an extension and they start going off at you, claiming that they gave you more than enough time, asking you why you couldn't manage your time properly, questioning your skills and work ethic. Starting to get mad? Of course you are, who wouldn't? It's not like you didn't *try* to complete the task and it's certainly not a case of you not being capable enough to manage your workload. It's just that forces outside of your control caused you to fall behind. If only your boss had stopped to consider that you may have a legitimate reason for being behind before going off at you. If they had, maybe you could have talked it out and found a solution to the problem without getting into a screaming match.

However, before you get angry at your boss's unreasonable behavior and start screaming at them, try taking a moment to consider *their* feelings. Perhaps *they* have been under a lot of pressure from *their* boss to complete a project that depends on the completion of your task. Perhaps *they* are going through some personal issues themselves, which is causing them added stress. Perhaps they have just been having a really bad day and are speaking without thinking.

Empathy is a two-way street and while you cannot always count on the other person to exercise empathy, if you yourself can take the time to put yourself in their shoes, it is a step in the right direction. Exercising empathy will always help in facilitating positive communication. "When you approach the other person with empathy, you quell the tendency to respond to inappropriate anger with anger of your own" (Zetlin, 2020). Taking the time to understand the other person's emotions will not only stop a conflict from escalating out of control, it will allow you to understand your own anger and help you communicate yourself and your needs more clearly. Hopefully, this will allow the other person to understand you better and together you can reach common ground and build a stronger bond.

STRATEGIZE BEFORE YOU REACT

Getting angry may be an automatic reaction, but the actions taken out of anger should never be automatic. Developing and exercising your EQ will allow you to recognize and understand your anger, then allow you to take a step back and implement strategies to regulate your anger and choose the best course of action to arrive at a positive outcome.

Anger comes with a variety of warning signs, both physical and mental. The warning signs associated with anger differ between individuals. Recognizing your own warning signs is the first step to managing your anger.

The next step is to find the anger management strategies that work for you. Just how the way in which we exhibit anger differs between individuals, so too do the strategies that are effective in managing anger. There are a whole host of anger management strategies out there and just because one strategy works for someone doesn't necessarily mean that it will work for you. Your particular type of anger may not respond to meditation but may respond really well to physical exercise. In order to find the right anger management strategy for you, you need to first understand what type of anger is typical to you, then experiment with strategies until you find one that works.

Once you have found an anger management strategy that works for you, use it. Put it into practice as soon as you start feeling yourself getting angry. It's important to remember that the goal of anger management strategies is not to suppress the emotion. No matter what you do, you will still get angry sometimes and this is a normal and healthy way to live. You can't, and shouldn't, get rid of anger or the sources of your anger. The goal of anger management strategies is to control the intensity of the feeling so that you don't react to it instinctively, potentially lashing out at the cause of your anger. The goal is for you to manage your anger and get to a state where you can be honest and objective about it, able to truthfully answer questions like, "Is my anger justified?" or, "How are my actions affecting those around me?" and, "What is the best thing to do from here?"

Once you have reached this state of mind, you will be more able to strategize and come up with a course of action that will be beneficial for yourself and for those around you. You will no longer be a slave to your anger and you will be able to make it work for you, using it as a tool to take assertive action rather than aggressive action.

Chapter 2: Understanding Your Anger, Part 1

There have been a lot of studies done on anger and the emotion has been defined in many different ways throughout these studies. In order to control your anger, it is necessary to understand your anger; not just what motivates the emotion but how your mind typically processes and expresses the emotion. Different things trigger anger in different people. Similarly, the emotion can be processed and expressed in a multitude of ways that vary depending on your disposition. In order to find a strategy that best manages your anger type, it is important for you to first identify what type of anger you possess.

THE SIX DIMENSIONS OF ANGER

Professor Ephrem Fernandez (2016) proposes that there are six main dimensions in the expression of anger and each of these dimensions is anchored by a pair of distinct markers. These dimensions of anger cover how a person typically expresses their anger, whether they choose to bottle it, verbalize it, or express it physically. They also cover how well the anger is controlled, as well as the ultimate goal of the anger.

Each dimension is expressed in a sliding scale, which is to say people seldom only demonstrate only one anchor at all times. You might consider yourself to be very open about your anger, but there still might be situations where you find yourself bottling up the anger rather than verbalizing it. You might be the type that seeks to punish people that make you angry, but when dealing with someone close to you, someone who you can't bring yourself to harming, you may decide to take a restorative approach rather than a punitive approach. The scale of each dimension seeks to measure how prone you are to a particular expression of anger versus another. How likely are you to direct your anger inward versus directing it outwards? How likely are you to verbalize your anger as opposed to expressing it physically?

Theoretically, these dimensions of anger are independent of each other. There is no point on any particular scale that will dictate where you land on another scale; there are patterns of behavior that can be observed. For example, if you are the type of person who is prone to expressing your anger physically, it is likely that you are also the type of person to direct your anger outwards rather than inwards. However, this is not an absolute. Every person feels, processes, and expresses anger differently and it is because of this that the dimensions are divided as such, in order to accommodate as many possible combinations as the human mind can produce.

In this chapter we will go through each dimension and its two anchors in order for you to get a better idea of what type of anger you possess. As you're going through each dimension, ask yourself honestly which end of the scale you fall at for each. There are no wrong or right answers to this and the goal is not for you to feel judged. The goal is simply for you to understand your own anger and what form it takes, so that you are better equipped to recognize your own anger when it comes and find a strategy that helps you control it.

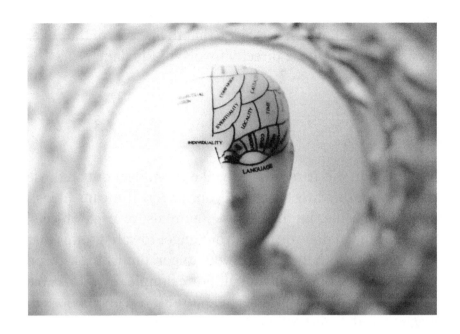

DIMENSION I: ANGER DIRECTION

This dimension asks you: Where do you typically direct your anger? Who is the target of your anger? When you are wronged, do you strike back at the person that wronged you or do you take it out on those around you? The two anchors of this dimension are reflection and deflection.

REFLECTION

Reflection, in this case, means to reciprocate. It means to hit back, to give as good as you got, an eye for an eye. It means that you direct your anger at the person that you feel wronged you. The degree at which you pay the person back can vary. The distinction is that the anger is focused on one target—the one who wronged you. This can create a vicious cycle wherein you pay back the person that wronged you, who then pays you back in kind, causing you to return the favor, and so on. However, given that the targets of the anger are restricted to those directly involved, the damage can be contained.

DEFLECTION

Deflection in this case means to take your anger out on those that are not the direct cause of your anger. It means to lash out at innocents, be they people, animals, or even objects. This may mean that you direct your anger toward groups that you associate with the cause of your anger, punishing a group for the actions of an individual. For example, if you receive poor service from a waiter at a restaurant, you may choose to never visit that restaurant again and give a negative review, even though the owner and the rest of the staff may be perfectly nice people. Sometimes deflection occurs when the source of your anger is perceived to be untargetable. A classic example of this is if when you are yelled at by your boss at work, rather than yelling back at them, which may damage your career, you choose to take it out on your family once you get home. You transfer your anger to a target that you believe will cause fewer long-term repercussions.

DIMENSION II: ANGER LOCUS

This dimension seeks to ask, where does your anger live? Do you wear your anger on your sleeve or do you keep it buried deep inside you? Can you keep a poker face or are you an open book? The two anchors of this dimension are internalization and externalization.

INTERNALIZATION

Internalization is a form of emotional suppression. It means to keep your anger hidden from view, bottling up inside you. This is often done in an attempt to avoid harming others. You believe that getting angry and yelling at someone may hurt their feelings, so you choose to swallow your anger and hold your tongue. It can also be done to avoid embarrassing yourself. If you get angry in a public place you may believe that causing a scene would only cause further embarrassment, so you suppress the emotion and delay your outburst to a more appropriate time and forum. You may even choose to internalize your anger so that the object of your anger will be caught unaware when you eventually take revenge. Depending on how good you are at concealing your feelings, it may be possible that the target of your anger is completely unaware of how you're feeling. That is, until the effort of concealing the anger proves too great and the proverbial dam breaks, releasing your fury to the outside world.

EXTERNALIZATION

Externalized anger is an outward expression of anger. The degree and nature of its expression can vary from person to person. It could be expressed in a subtle or unsubtle facial expression or it could be vocalized by the angered person. It could even be expressed in physical actions such as pacing, or balling your hands into fists. At the worst of times it is expressed by acts of violence, such as throwing things, punching, or kicking. The greater the anger, the more likely it is to be expressed outwardly. Externalized anger can be the result of internalized anger becoming too great for the bearer to keep inside, causing them to snap. However, there are some people that are just open about their anger and choose to let people know when they are angry. There are even those that simply can't hide it, even if they try. It is always apparent when they are angry by their face and mannerisms.

DIMENSION III: ANGER REACTION

This dimension refers to how you typically react when angry, specifically toward the cause of your anger. This dimension can best be explained with the following scenario: it's the evening before garbage collection day. You take your bins to the curb and you notice that your bin is fuller than usual. You open it up and see that your bin has been filled up to the top but not by your own trash. You look over at your neighbor's bin and see that it is filled to the top with similar colored garbage bags. It is apparent that your neighbor has had a trash-heavy week and has decided, with their bin being too full to fit any more garbage, to place their garbage in your bin instead. Immediately, you become angry. They've come onto your property and put garbage in your bin without your permission. How are you more likely to respond to this anger? For the sake of demonstrating this dimension of anger you have two choices. You could put a lock on your bin, so that if your neighbor tries to do it again he won't be able to. Alternatively, you could respond in kind and start putting your own garbage in your neighbor's bin this week. Which would you choose?

RESISTANCE

You've chosen to put a lock on your bin. If your neighbor tries to put their garbage in your bin again, they will see that it is locked and realize that you have caught on to their game. You've expressed your anger with defiance rather than aggression. This reaction to anger is referred to as resistance, but it is also known commonly as passive-aggression. In this scenario, the resistant action takes the form of defiance, but passive-aggression can be expressed in a variety of ways, such as procrastination, disengagement, or non-compliance. If you are angry with your workload, you may choose to procrastinate. If you are angry with your friend, you may choose to not speak to them. If you are angry with the government, you may choose a path of civil-disobedience. All of these responses are a resistant reaction to anger and while the results of such responses may not be as obvious as those of a more retaliatory response, they may still be damaging to the parties involved. A worker strike can be just as damaging to a company as active protests; that is why it gets results and why many unions choose striking as a desired course of action.

RETALIATION

Retaliation means responding in kind. Counter-attacking. If you're more on the retaliation end of the scale you are more likely to want to return your neighbor's actions by putting your own garbage in *their* bin. Your neighbor will likely notice what you are doing, connect the dots as to *why* you are doing it and will be presented with the choice to either stop dumping in your bin or retaliate to your actions. Bear in mind that in this example scenario, while the action taken is more retaliatory than putting a lock on your bin, it is still fairly passive when compared to other possible examples. In its truest sense, a retaliatory reaction to anger means punching back when punched. This reaction could cause your opponent to retaliate in kind, which would then spiral into a full-blown fight, where damage is sustained by both parties. On a global scale, this kind of reaction can lead to open war, causing catastrophe beyond measure.

DIMENSION IV: ANGER MODALITY

This dimension of anger refers to how you typically express your anger, verbally or physically. Are you more prone to swearing under your breath or frowning? Are you more likely to stare daggers at someone who has angered you or start screaming at them? When something has ticked you off, do you tend to utter a sound of annoyance or shake your head in frustration? It is important to understand that these two markers are not mutually exclusive. Most people will exhibit both verbal and physical expressions of anger, possibly simultaneously. In some cases, a physical expression may be used to reinforce a verbal expression of anger. For example, if you are getting angry at your young child for constantly reaching for a candy bar that they know is not for them, you might tell them to stop, using an angry tone to let them know that this behavior is unacceptable, but you might also slap their hand away to reinforce the lesson that they are doing the wrong thing. Since verbal responses and physical responses are often expressed concurrently, the question becomes which response is more automatic for you.

VERBAL

A verbal response to anger is auditory in nature. A verbal response can take the form of a statement of blame, a sarcastic remark, or an expletive. It doesn't necessarily refer to specific words spoken but rather the tone at which they are spoken. When people are angry they tend to speak in a higher pitch, at a louder volume, a faster tempo, and with a coarser tone, though this is not always the case. There are several possible combinations of content and acoustics. If angered, you may be prone to softly-spoken sarcastic remarks or you may be prone to shouting profanities. Regardless of the nature of the response, you have chosen to express it verbally.

PHYSICAL

Physical responses to anger are also varied. A contortion of the face like the simple act of frowning would be considered a physical response to anger. Even subtle facial ticks could be considered as such. More obvious physical responses could be seen in body movements such as pacing, stomping, changing postures, or aggressive hand gestures. Of course, the physical responses that are the most obvious and the most destructive are acts of violence such as pushing and striking. While verbal responses can be destructive at a psychological level, violence can inflict physical harm on others.

DIMENSION V: ANGER IMPULSIVITY

This dimension refers to how skilled you are at regulating your anger. How quick are you to act on your anger? Is anger a knee-jerk reaction for you or are you able to pause long enough to control your anger? Are you reflexive or reflective? Considering that you are reading this book, it is probably safe to assume that you are more toward the uncontrolled side of the scale. That's okay. Everybody struggles with controlling anger and the subject has been the basis of philosophical, theological, and psychological studies since time immemorial. Despite the amount of research that has been done on anger control, it is extremely rare to find someone who is completely on the controlled end of the scale.

CONTROLLED

Anger control doesn't refer to internalized anger, where the anger is suppressed and hidden within. Nor does it mean the total elimination of the emotion itself. It refers to the ability to keep your anger within reason and keep it from causing damage, whether it be physical damage or psychological damage inflicted on either yourself or others. It is the ability to stop and reflect upon yourself. The ability and desire to consider other people's feelings, consider how your actions would affect them, and brainstorming alternative solutions. If you are able to do this and adapt your thoughts to reach a positive outcome, this means that you have successfully controlled your anger.

UNCONTROLLED

Acting without thinking is what constitutes uncontrolled anger. It is allowing your anger to control your actions rather than taking action to control your anger. A person who exhibits purely uncontrolled anger doesn't stop to consider the other person's feelings or the consequences of their actions. They either act or react automatically or, in some cases, they are *compelled* to act. It's important to note that the action taken in anger may not necessarily be physical in nature. For example, you might lash out verbally in anger, uttering a harsh comment at the target of your anger. Looking back, you may not even have meant what you said. You just couldn't stop yourself from saying it. This type of uncontrolled response, while not causing any physical harm, still has potential for causing psychological harm to its target and damaging the bond between yourself and that person.

DIMENSION VI: ANGER OBJECTIVE

This dimension of anger asks: What do you seek to gain as a result of your anger? What is your goal? To see where you fall on this scale, let's present another hypothetical situation. You're eating at a restaurant in your local area. The restaurant is fairly new and it is the first time you are eating there. You're quite hungry, so when it takes a long time for your food to arrive you start to feel a little irate. You ask the waiter what the delay is and they apologize and say your food will be out in a few minutes. Sure enough, a dish arrives at your table a few minutes later. However, it is not the dish that you ordered. You complain to the waiter, who checks with the kitchen, then apologizes and tells you that the kitchen made a mistake and that they are making your dish now but it will take a bit longer. Hungry and angry, you tell the waiter that you will eat the dish that you have been given, despite it not being what you ordered. Once you have finished your meal and received the bill, the owner of the restaurant comes to your table and apologizes for the mistake. They offer you a discount and give you the meal you actually ordered in a takeaway box, free of charge. What do you do next? For the sake of demonstrating this dimension, you have two options. You can either accept the restaurant owner's apology, discount, and free meal and leave it at that. Alternatively, you can go home and relay your terrible dining experience to your family, then to your coworkers the next day at work, and to your friends after work, advising them all to never eat at that restaurant.

RESTORATIVE

You chose to accept the owner's apology, discount, and free meal and leave it at that. Let bygones be bygones. This means that your goal is restoration. If you are on the restorative end of this scale, you typically seek to get over your anger by arriving at an outcome where balance is maintained and both parties are satisfied. This could be achieved by you receiving an apology, compensation, or another form of reparation. A person on the far end of the restorative scale will still try to get over their anger even if reparation is not received. They are so committed to moving on from their anger that they will choose to forgive the restaurant and its staff without having received so much as an apology. Of course, this would still depend on the nature and degree of the offense.

PUNITIVE

You chose to bad mouth the restaurant to anyone who would listen, tarnishing their reputation and potentially damaging their business prospects, despite their efforts to repair the damage caused to you. This means that your desires are more punitive. People at this end of the scale are more inclined to continue feeling angry until they feel that the person or organization that has aggrieved them has been punished sufficiently. They are less likely to feel less angry even when compensation is offered. Their ability to forgive and forget is lower than those on the restorative end of the scale and they are more fixated on retribution.

Chapter 3: Understanding Your Anger, Part 2

You should be starting to get a better gauge of the precise nature of your anger; where it is located, how it is expressed, how in control of it you are, and what kind of goal you seek to achieve from it. Hopefully you will have been able to pinpoint which side of the scale you fall on for each of the six dimensions of anger. Next, we are going to examine the 10 most common types of anger; how they are displayed and how they can be controlled.

THE 10 MOST COMMON TYPES OF ANGER

As discussed in the previous chapter, there are lots of different combinations of anger modes. No one experiences anger quite the same as any other person. You could be someone who screams and yells at someone who makes you angry but quickly forgives and forgets as soon as they've apologized. You could be someone who keeps your anger bottled inside but secretly hopes that the person that made you angry receives karmic justice in the form of a terrible accident. You could be a passive aggressive person that chooses to direct your anger at the world as a whole, being sullen and uncooperative with everyone and everything.

While the specific experience of anger may be unique to each individual, there are trends that result in common types of anger. These will be addressed in the following list. Even if the way that you experience anger isn't covered in this list, you will be able to see similarities in them that you can relate to, and in recognizing these similarities, you will be one step closer to identifying the anger management strategy that will work for you.

In order to make this list as accessible as possible, I will propose an example scenario and each anger type will be represented by a response to this situation typical of a person who possesses that type.

The scenario is simple: you have been turned down for a promotion in favor of someone with less experience and tenure in your company. You have worked long and hard for this promotion, only to be denied it without explanation. You are angry, perhaps rightly so. The question is, how do you express your anger?

ASSERTIVE ANGER

WHAT DOES IT LOOK LIKE?

If you possess assertive anger, in response to missing out on the promotion you will stop and ask yourself why you were turned down for the promotion and how you can improve in order to be considered next time. You may even go so far as to approach your boss and ask for feedback in order to improve. This is the most constructive type of anger expression. Feelings of frustration and anguish are used as a catalyst for positive change. Anger is confronted, analyzed objectively, and acted upon with strategy and aforethought. If you exhibit this type of anger, you are able to express it without causing damage or distress to those around you.

HOW DO I CONTROL IT?

Assertive anger is a type of controlled anger. It is defined by being in control as long as you are using it toward positive results such as overcoming fear, addressing injustice, or achieving a desired outcome.

CHRONIC ANGER

WHAT DOES IT LOOK LIKE?

If you possess chronic anger, in response to missing out on the promotion you will become resentful toward your boss, your job, your coworkers, and even toward your friends and family. This type of anger is ongoing and is usually internalized but quick to make an appearance if you're provoked. It is a constant feeling of frustration; frustration with yourself, those around you, or your current circumstances. It can stem from a general feeling of not being in control of your situation, which leads to feelings of hopelessness that are expressed as perpetual irritability. This type of prolonged anger can impact your health and wellbeing negatively.

HOW DO I CONTROL IT?

You should stop and ask yourself what the cause of your anger is. Once the cause of your anger has been identified, you should take steps to resolving the conflict, either inside yourself or in your current situation. This may mean finding the strength to forgive whoever you feel has wronged you, or communicating your feelings clearly and constructively to the party or parties responsible so that you can come to a mutual understanding. Whichever positive avenue you choose to deal with your anger, dealing with it will allow you to let it go and prevent it from continuing to brew inside you.

BEHAVIORAL ANGER

WHAT DOES IT LOOK LIKE?

If you possess behavioral anger, in response to missing out on the promotion you will feel the need to react physically. You may respond to the news by breaking something in the office, whether it be something small like a pencil or something large like a computer. You may feel the need to scrunch up a piece of paper and aggressively throw it into the wastebasket. However, if you demonstrate an extreme type of behavioral anger, you may act aggressively toward your boss and/or coworkers. It's even possible for you to become violent toward these people. Behavioral anger is a type of anger that causes you to lash out physically; to express your anger with physical, typically aggressive, actions. It goes without saying that these actions can cause physical harm to those around you, but the volatile and uncontrolled nature of your behavior can negatively impact your ability to form lasting bonds with people, as it will cause people to distrust you.

HOW DO I CONTROL IT?

While a physical response to anger is quite often aggressive in nature, it's important to note that anger doesn't automatically lead to aggression or violence. Consider some self-reflection and try to figure out why you are choosing aggression as an outlet for your anger. If you are unable to do this, try to at least identify the warning signs of your aggressive behavior. As soon as you feel yourself exhibiting these warning signs, try to step away from the situation that is causing the anger, or manage it by telling yourself to stay calm. Actually say the words out loud and couple it with some of the deep breathing and muscle relaxation techniques that we will cover further in this book. If these fail and you still feel the need to express your anger physically, take up an active but constructive hobby like working out or running.

VERBAL ANGER

WHAT DOES IT LOOK LIKE?

If you possess verbal anger, in response to missing out on the promotion you will seek to hurt your boss with words. You may shout at them, criticize them, ridicule them, whatever you think would hurt them the most. You will also most likely turn on your savage tongue on the coworker that was promoted ahead of you as well as anyone else that gets in the way of your tirade. Verbal anger is similar to behavioral anger in that the anger is expressed with acts of aggression that are intended to cause harm to whatever or whoever is making you angry. However, in the case of verbal anger, the harm inflicted is psychological in nature, rather than physical.

HOW DO I CONTROL IT?

Breathe. Before saying anything, just breathe. The trick to controlling verbal anger is to delay your response long enough for you to prevent yourself from verbalizing your first thought, because that first thought is bound to be vicious. The good thing about this type of anger is that your first reaction is verbal rather than physical, so you are already prone to expressing your anger with your words rather than your fists. If you are able to stop yourself from vocalizing your first thought, you will be one step closer to being able to replace your tendency to resort to verbal abuse with a more constructive verbal expression of anger.

JUDGMENTAL ANGER

WHAT DOES IT LOOK LIKE?

If you possess judgmental anger, in response to missing out on the promotion you are likely to start bad-mouthing the parties involved and disparaging their worth. You might call your boss an idiot who doesn't know what they're doing. You might say that the coworker that was promoted ahead of you is laughably unqualified for the position and that they won't last a week. You may say that the company you work for is beneath you and that you're better off working for a company that recognizes your talents. Or you may say that the whole system is unfair and give up on any further opportunities to rise up the ranks. Judgmental anger stems from a core belief that you are better than, or less than, others. It is usually the reaction of indignation to a perceived injustice or someone else's perceived shortcomings. The problem with judgmental anger is that no matter how justified your complaints may be, they will only result in you pushing people away because you will constantly assume that the opinions of others are less valid than your own.

HOW DO I CONTROL IT?

The best way to manage judgmental anger is to exercise empathy and try to understand other people's viewpoints. While you may disagree with someone's opinion, by trying to see things from their point of view, you are opening yourself up to other perspectives and potentially gaining insights that will give you more ideas on how to arrive at a positive solution. If you can do this, you will get the added bonus of people looking favorably upon you as you will have less of a tendency to come across as condescending or belittling.

PASSIVE-AGGRESSIVE ANGER

WHAT DOES IT LOOK LIKE?

If you possess passive-aggressive anger, in response to missing out on the promotion you are likely to put less effort into your work going forward, procrastinating or delivering lack-lustre results. You may even become uncooperative at work, particularly when dealing with your boss or the coworker that was promoted ahead of you. A passive-aggressive person tends to avoid expressing their anger outright and prefers to more subtle methods of venting such as non-compliance, sarcasm, or veiled mockery. A passive-aggressive person will typically feel that this type of anger expression is less damaging than active-aggression. They may even not see their behavior as aggressive at all. However, people on the receiving end of passive-aggression usually notice the change in behavior and this will cause feelings of confusion and frustration. Often they will wish that the angry person would just confront them, rather than being passive-aggressive.

HOW DO I CONTROL IT?

The key for controlling passive-aggression is communication. Practice the assertive communication techniques that we will cover later in this book. Usually passive-aggression is born from a fear of confrontation. Try exploring this fear within yourself and little by little work on articulating your frustrations to your close friends and relatives. Try analyzing the situation that is making you frustrated and using cognitive restructuring to come up with strategies for voicing your anger without damaging relationships. With every successful exchange, you will see your confidence grow and your fear of confrontation melt away.

OVERWHELMED ANGER

WHAT DOES IT LOOK LIKE?

If you possess overwhelmed anger, in response to missing out on the promotion you will not be able to control yourself. You may break down and start crying. You may need to go somewhere private and scream your lungs out. You may need to rush to the bathroom to vomit. Whatever form the response takes, it will be uncontrolled. Overwhelmed anger usually occurs when you feel that you don't have control over your situation or circumstances. It is commonly experienced by people that have taken on more responsibility than they can handle or people that have been affected negatively by unexpected events. It occurs when a person feels more stress than their mind can handle. Their mind is so full of negative thoughts that one additional trigger, even a small one, will result in a response that is strong and sudden.

HOW DO I CONTROL IT?

If you are experiencing overwhelmed anger you need to reach out for support. Find people to talk to, whether they are family members, friends, or coworkers. You don't necessarily have to tell them how you're feeling, as long as you can ask them to provide you with some help and support to lighten your burden. Your life is probably so jam-packed with obligations that you can barely have time to yourself. Balancing work, family, and a social life can be a nightmare and is bound to cause stress. By asking for help you can trim down the list of things to do, giving yourself more time and alleviating potential sources of stress. Ask your partner to cook dinner every Wednesday night so that you can have one night a week away from the stove. Ask your coworker to help you with your paperwork so that you take your time completing your other work. Ask your best friend to babysit every now and then so that you can have a night to yourself. Trim down your to-do list where you can and don't feel that you need to carry the entire weight of your world on your shoulders.

SELF-ABUSIVE ANGER

WHAT DOES IT LOOK LIKE?

If you possess self-abusive anger, in response to missing out on the promotion you will tell yourself that you didn't deserve the promotion and you were stupid to even have applied. You will swear at yourself and may even try to punish yourself with self-inflicted harm. Self-abusive anger stems from feelings of humiliation, shame, and unworthiness. It is typically expressed internally with negative self-talk and self-harm. Physical self-harm is particularly dangerous and can be represented in the form of self-inflicted wounds, drug use, alcoholism, or disordered eating. Self-abusive anger has many similarities to clinical depression, though anger tends to spark action rather than inaction.

HOW DO I CONTROL IT?

The best way to manage self-abusive anger is to change the way you think. If your anger is self-abusive, it means you have a tendency toward thoughts of self-defeat. Exercising cognitive reframing techniques is a good way to transform these kinds of thoughts into more objective thoughts. By learning to be objective, you will soon see that you are not always to blame, that other factors may be responsible for a situation that is causing you anguish. Once you become better at being objective, you will be able to stop punishing yourself and think of more constructive ways to address the situation.

RETALIATORY ANGER

WHAT DOES IT LOOK LIKE?

If you possess retaliatory anger, in response to missing out on the promotion you will become extremely defensive. You will attack your boss verbally and demand an explanation. You will attack the coworker that was promoted ahead of you and list all the reasons why you are better suited for the position. You may even quit your job. Retaliatory anger is an automatic and instinctive response to feelings of confrontation or aggression. It is the need to fight back at those that have wronged you. In the case of the above scenario, you would feel that your professional abilities have been attacked and you will seek to defend these abilities while at the same time punishing those that have called them into question. Retaliatory anger is the most common type of anger and while the resultant act of vengeance may not necessarily be deliberate, it often leads to escalation when retaliation is reciprocated in kind.

HOW DO I CONTROL IT?

Stopping to think is often enough to control relatialiatory anger and prevent it from escalating. If you can pause long enough to think about the consequences of your actions, you may be able to remember the last time you got angry, what you did in response to that anger, and those actions resulted in a positive outcome. It is rare that a problematic situation is resolved with a cycle of retribution. By recognizing this fact, you will be more likely to reexamine your actions and take a different approach.

VOLATILE ANGER

WHAT DOES IT LOOK LIKE?

If you possess volatile anger, in response to missing out on the promotion you will curse loudly and slam your fist on the table, then calm down almost immediately. The coworkers around you will look over briefly before hastily getting back to work, too scared to check to see if you're okay. People who possess volatile anger are quick to anger but often calm down just as quickly. This may sound okay but being quick to anger, even at the smallest of annoyances, makes it difficult for you to maintain close relationships with those around you. People will become scared of you or feel the need to tread very carefully in your presence for fear of enraging you. This will generally make people not want to be around you.

HOW DO I CONTROL IT?

The best thing for you to do is try to identify the warning signs of your outbursts. As soon as you sense an outburst coming, use deep breathing, go to your happy place, or remove yourself from the situation to stop your anger from escalating. If you don't manage to succeed in stopping the outburst and it slips out, don't ignore it. Apologize to the people around you for your outburst and promise that it won't happen again. This will show them that you recognize the negative behavior and that you are at least trying to get a handle on it.

Chapter 4:
In the Heat of the
Moment

Now that we've taken a deep dive into the different types of anger and modes of anger expression, hopefully you've been able to identify which type of anger is most typical to you. Next, let's talk about how to minimize the immediate negative effects of your anger.

One thing that most anger types have in common is the moment at which the anger is the strongest. Usually the emotion of anger is strongest felt immediately after the trigger is experienced. The moment directly after someone has insulted you, or backed into your car, or cut in front of you in line, is the time that you will tend to feel the angriest. This is the moment when you are likely to speak or act without thinking. This is perhaps the most crucial moment in terms of getting your anger under control. Unfortunately, it is also the moment where you happen to be in the least control.

Anger is a fire that burns brightly and quickly. We need to be able to take control of it the moment it flares up in order to prevent it from spreading. This chapter will highlight various ways to recognize the warning signs of your anger as well as some quick solutions to manage your anger at the initial flare up, when it has the most potential to cause damage.

RECOGNIZING THE WARNING SIGNS

In order to be in a position to control your anger when it occurs, you need to be able to recognize when you're getting angry. This relates to the self-awareness category of emotional intelligence. What makes anger a particularly difficult emotion to detect initially is that the emotion itself can cloud your judgment and cause you to be less objective, especially during the initial spark. However, there are common tell-tale signs that take place when a person starts to feel angry. The human body undergoes several neurological and physiological changes when put under the stress of anger. If you are aware of these changes and are able to recognize them as they happen, you will be in a better position to control your anger in the early stages.

PHYSICAL SIGNS

Anger is an emotion that has been genetically passed down by our ancestors. Its purpose is to prepare the human body to deal with threats. As such, when an outside force sparks the emotion of anger, the body's "fight-or-flight" response is triggered, causing several physiological changes.

Here is a breakdown of what happens to your brain and body when you get angry. The first spark of anger triggers a part of your brain called the amygdala. The amygdala activates the hypothalamus, which is responsible for regulating hormone release. Corticotropin-releasing hormone (CRH) is discharged from the hypothalamus, signalling the pituitary gland to activate the adrenal glands. Once activated, the adrenal glands begin to secrete stress hormones like cortisol, adrenaline, and noradrenaline. All of this happens before you're even aware that you're angry.

The purpose of these hormones is to prepare the body for either fighting off or fleeing from threats. They cause blood to be diverted from the gut to the muscles, in preparation for physical exertion. As a result of this, your heart rate, blood pressure, and respiration will increase. This increased blood flow will make your body temperature rise, which in turn causes your body to sweat. If you've ever been so angry that it "made your blood boil," this chain reaction occurring inside your body is the reason for feeling that way.

The good news is that these internal changes come with visible cues. These cues will give you a good indication of when you are starting to experience anger, even if your judgment has been clouded. As mentioned above, your heart will start pounding as blood is pumped through your body at a faster rate. You will begin to sweat, particularly on your palms. You may also start to feel hot, especially in your face and neck. This is also a side effect of the increased blood flow.

The chemical responses caused by anger may also have an effect on your muscles. Your brain diverts blood to your muscles, activating them involuntarily. This can cause uncontrollable shaking or trembling, hence the saying "trembling with rage." Since blood is being diverted from your gut, you may also suffer from stomachaches or nausea. You may literally become sick with anger.

Anger has even been known to cause headaches and migraines. These headaches are generally called tension headaches, but they can be caused by a number of reactions to anger, such as increased blood pressure, changes in hormone levels, and muscle tension around the neck and scalp.

If you are experiencing any of these physical changes, you may want to take a step back and examine your emotional state. Odds are you are starting to get angry, even if you're not fully aware of it yet.

It's also important to note that the more anger pent up inside, the stronger these physical signs seem to be. Chronic anger will lead to increased levels of the stress hormone cortisol. Too much cortisol will decrease serotonin, the hormone responsible for making you happy. Decreased serotonin levels can make you feel anger more easily and can also increase your level of aggression. Furthermore, because of the stress anger causes on the heart, chronic anger can lead to health issues such as increased blood pressure, increased blood glucose levels, clogged or damaged blood vessels, and even strokes or heart attacks. This highlights the importance of being able to express your anger in a healthy manner.

EMOTIONAL SIGNS

The stress hormones involved in anger can also cause changes to our emotional state. In this way, anger can be an instigator of other negative emotions, mostly related to stress. Frustration, irritation, and resentment are offshoots of anger, of course, but anger can also lead to emotions like sadness, guilt, anxiousness, and depression.

Usually it is suppressed anger that will lead to the latter emotions and it is because of a part of your brain called the amygdala. It is here where anger is initially registered and where the ensuing internal chain reaction begins. However, the amygdala is not only responsible for registering and responding to anger, it is also responsible for regulating a range of other emotions. Because of this, the mind, particularly a turbulent mind like that of someone experiencing chronic anger, can sometimes mix emotions together or get them confused.

Along with anger, the amygdala is also the source of feelings defined as disappointment and rejection. If your amygdala is overworked due to chronic anger, you may start to feel these emotions in conjunction with anger. This is why the act of crying can sometimes be associated with anger. You will also find it harder to feel happy due to the decrease in serotonin levels and the increase in cortisol. This can lead to depression.

The amygdala is also responsible for the emotion of fear. This is where anxiousness comes in. The fight or flight response triggered in the amygdala by outside threats also applies to fear. While the "fight" part of the response is the typical reaction to anger and can cause aggressive behavior, the "flight" part of the response is more closely linked to fear and causes the desire to flee. When these two emotions are overworked, it can cause the two to become confused. This is why you may begin to feel anxious when you start to become angry and you may feel a strong urge to flee from the situation that is causing you anger.

The feeling of judgment also springs from the amygdala. Judgment is related to guilt. In the case of guilt it is a form of self-judgment; the sense that you are unworthy, deserving of these negative feelings, or somehow responsible for the situation that caused them.

If you respond to a situation that should be causing you anger by instead feeling guilty, anxious, sad, or depressed, you may want to take a step back to reexamine your emotions. It's possible that you are feeling angry and that chronic anger is causing these emotions to come out in different ways.

TELLTALE ACTIONS

Along with the physical and emotional signs of anger, there are a range of behavior patterns that are typical to people experiencing anger. This is because the body will instinctively react to the changes taking place within the body and mind. It is likely that when you are angry, you may perform the following acts without even realizing that you are doing so.

Raising your voice or yelling is a typical response to anger and it is part of the fight or flight response. Increased aggression that manifests itself in loud vocal tones is an instinctive response designed to scare away would-be threats. It is similar to a dog's bark or a lion's roar. The difference in humans is that we have the gift of language, so we are able to vocalize our thoughts into intelligible speech. However, the instinct to vocalize these thoughts in a loud and aggressive tone is purely instinct. Furthermore, elevated cortisol levels negatively affect the prefrontal cortex, causing a loss of neurons and preventing you from using your best judgment. This explains why angry people tend to act irrationally and find it difficult to articulate their anger well. Cortisol also suppresses activity in the hippocampus, which is responsible for short-term memory. This is why you may find it difficult to recall exactly what you said during a heated argument.

Pacing and clenching your fists are also typical acts of a person experiencing anger. Actions such as these are caused by the increased blood flow to your muscles, again, caused by the fight or flight response. Because your muscles are being activated in preparation for physical exertion, your body will have the urge to utilize these muscles. If you happen to be in the midst of an argument where it would be unnatural behavior to flee, your body will seek to move around as much as it can while still maintaining socially normal standards of behavior. This will lead to the automatic reaction of pacing or making fists. If anger is in an uncontrolled state, it may lead to you lashing out physically.

Cravings can also occur when anger is triggered. Craving substances that relax you such as alcohol, cigarettes, or food is a natural response to anger. In the case of alcohol, it is because alcohol acts as a pain inhibitor. Drinking alcohol releases endorphins that bind certain receptors in the brain, causing pain to lessen and pleasure to increase. If you are under stress or feeling angry, your body may crave alcohol in order to numb the pain caused by negative emotions.

In the case of food cravings, the body is responding to changing blood-glucose levels caused by the sudden increase in blood pressure. Blood-glucose levels may increase in a state of anger, but as the anger subsides and blood pressure begins to normalize, these levels decrease again just as sharply. Your body will seek to level out your blood-glucose levels, leading to the craving for food.

Many people will crave a cigarette when angry and there have been numerous studies on the cause of this. One such study was performed by Mustafa al'Absi (2007), who sought to find a correlation between high levels of anger and the risk of relapse among smokers seeking to quit. The experiment involved a test group of chronic smokers of different backgrounds and different levels of trait anger. The test group was made to abstain from smoking for a 24-hour period, after which they performed a series of mental and social stress challenges under laboratory conditions. Saliva samples were collected during the 24-hour period to measure their cortisol levels throughout the experiment. Blood samples were also collected after the stress challenges were performed to measure adrenocorticotropin (ACTH) and cortisol levels. "The findings support the hypothesis that smokers high in anger trait may have greater mood difficulties during abstinence and may be more vulnerable to early relapse than smokers with low anger trait" (al'Absi et al., 2007).

This experiment shows us that anger and the release of the stress hormones cortisol and ACTH increases the urge to smoke, which makes it more difficult for angry people to quit smoking.

IMMEDIATE SOLUTIONS

Once you have become adept in recognizing the warning signs of your anger and registering the emotion on a cognitive level, you can take steps toward managing your anger. While managing anger is a long-term struggle with no fast-track solution, there are ways for you that you can curb your anger and put it out of your mind long enough to prevent you from taking action that may escalate a situation. These tactics are not meant as long-term solutions but rather band-aid solutions. Successfully implementing these may make you calm down during the initial emergence of anger but it is strongly advised that they be used in conjunction with more long-term measures in order to make sure that anger is being processed in a healthy way and not just being bottled.

COUNTING DOWN FROM (OR UP TO) 10

An oldy but a goody. This classic anger management strategy was famously advocated by former US president Thomas Jefferson who advised, "When angry, count to 10 before you speak. If very angry, a hundred."

It may sound simple but counting down from 10 or up to 10 is proven to work for a variety of reasons.

First, the act of counting triggers childhood memories of admonition in most people. Upon beginning the count, you will reflexively think of your childhood and how your parents used to implement the same strategy in order to calm you down as a child. You will subconsciously remember the repercussions of not calming down upon the conclusion of the count and this will incentivize your adult self to calm down.

Second, the act of counting provides a distraction for the mind. While counting, your mind is more concentrated on the number that comes next and less focused on your anger. Because your mind is busy counting, it is not actively adding fuel to the flames of your anger.

Third and perhaps most crucially, counting gives you time. It delays your immediate response, which more often than not would be a destructive response. This gives you time to gather your thoughts and think of a less damaging strategy to deal with your anger.

Counting in your head (or out loud) combines two key factors of anger management, time and distraction. Its effectiveness can be further increased by combining it with deep breathing exercises, which we will cover in Chapter 6 of this book.

People often associate the emotion anger with the color red, hence the popular adage "seeing red." When anger is sparked, it is not unusual for you to actually visualize the color red in your mind. In fact, studies have shown that angry people are more predisposed to choosing the color red during personality tests. One such study was performed by researchers at North Dakota State University. This study had a test group perform three tests to determine the link between personality, hostility, and colors.

The first test saw participants asked which color they preferred, red or blue, before completing a series of personality tests. Participants that presented hostile personalities generally opted for red.

In the second test, participants were shown a faded picture in which the dominant color could either be perceived as red or blue. They were asked which color they saw the picture as.

In the third test, participants were given a range of scenarios and asked what action they would take. Those who opted for hostile actions such as harming others always had a predisposition toward the color red. "Hostile thoughts are implicitly associated with the color red, and therefore hostile people are biased to see this color more frequently" (Evans, 2014).

There are many theories behind the connection of anger and the color red. One theory is that the connection stems from our ancient ancestors, who linked the color with danger such as poisonous plants, dangerous insects, or even the presence of blood.

There is also a correlation between hostility and biochemistry. People tend to flush red when angry. Several species of animals can attribute their red coloring to high levels of testosterone, a hormone responsible for increased aggression.

Whatever the reason, there is no doubt that the color red is linked to anger and much like a bull, you might feel inclined to charge upon seeing the color. However, in society the color red is also the universal signal to stop. A red traffic light generally means "Stop." Since the 1950s, all stop signs have been colored red. Even signs indicating no entry are usually colored red.

Next time you are angry enough to "see red," instead of associating the color with the charging of a bull, try picturing a stop sign in your mind. Upon seeing the stop sign, your body and mind will reflexively stop in their tracks, and you will be able to halt yourself long enough to prevent any damaging actions.

STRETCH YOUR BODY

As previously mentioned, anger causes an increase in blood flow to the muscles resulting in a surge of energy and a compulsion for physical movement. This is why physical exercise can prove an excellent strategy for managing anger, as moving your body around releases energy caused by the emotion, reducing the need for it to come out in acts of violence. Taking up hobbies like running, boxing, weightlifting, or yoga are all recommended forms of stress relief.

While these forms of physical exercise can be cathartic, they are not always practical at the immediate moment of anger. When in the middle of an argument, or stuck in traffic, or waiting for way too long for our coffee order, it would be weird for us to start sprinting, shadow-boxing, or dropping down and doing yoga stretches on the floor in order to relieve your angry energy.

However, there are other ways to relieve anger-related muscle tension without looking like a complete weirdo. Try doing some subtle stretching, particularly of your neck and shoulders. Neck and shoulder rolls are good examples of non-strenuous and subtle movements that can be good for calming down during the immediate instance of anger. They are movements that are similar to yoga stretches, but they are less noticeable to the people around you and less likely to draw attention than yoga stretches. Use these to calm yourself long enough for you to escape to the privacy of your own home, where you can follow them up with more vigorous activities to get rid of any residual feelings of anger.

REPEAT A MANTRA

A mantra is a formula, word, incantation, or prayer, often repeated as an object of concentration. It is originally a Sanskrit word that literally means "instrument of thought." Because the word mantra is often associated with meditation and chanting, people may mistake its use as a form of self-hypnosis or mind control. However, this is far from the truth.

Mantras are not about controlling one's thoughts, but rather recognizing and accepting how little control one has over one's thoughts. We can't control the way that we think or the way that we feel. However, what we can control is our awareness of our thoughts and feelings and our responses to them.

A mantra can be used to facilitate communication and understanding. In order to use it as a form of anger management, you need to understand that you are feeling angry and communicate with yourself using your mantra, telling yourself that you are angry and that you need to calm down. Find a word or phrase that helps you calm down and refocus. If you recognize that you're starting to feel angry, repeat these words to yourself over and over again until you start to calm down. The act of recalling and speaking the words will provide time and distraction, while the words themselves will serve as a reminder of what is important.

Here are some suggestions for mantras that can be effective in soothing anger.

1. **"Let it go."** Hanging on to resentment and anger can only lead to further damage. Letting go of your anger can be a powerful sentiment that reminds you to seek positive resolutions to your anger, rather than bottling it up inside.

2. **"Within me is a peacefulness that cannot be disturbed."** This is a mantra used by many who frequently practice meditation as a strategy for anger management. It seeks to remind the speaker that the calm attained through meditation is always present.
3. **"Breathing in I calm my body, breathing out I smile."** This mantra reinforces the idea that deep breaths can help us relax and putting on a smile can dramatically improve our mood.

Chapter 5: Communication

When we are angry with someone, it is natural to want to express this anger. In fact, it is healthy to let that person know that you are angry, rather than keeping it bottled up inside. However, problems arise when the emotion leads to negative communication. Think of the last time you got angry with someone. How did you express it? Did the conversation lead to a positive outcome?

Communication is complicated. It is complicated because it involves more than one person and each person may have a different style of communication. Some people are very reserved, while others are more open and expressive, like Stanley Ipkis before and after donning the titular Mask. Some people have a naturally loud voice like Tigger, while others tend to be more softly spoken like Pooh. Some people like to give long-winded speeches to get their point across, like Morpheus from the Matrix, while others manage to express themselves with one word sentences, more reminiscent of Neo. "Most of us tend to communicate in a way that was adaptive in the environment we grew up in" (*Assertive Communication: An Anger Management Technique*, n.d.). Someone who grew up with a family that expressed their emotions freely would be more inclined to open communication, whereas someone that grew up in a more reserved household may shy away from direct confrontation.

Communication styles that work for some people might be unpleasant for others. Let's say that you grew up in a loud household with many siblings, so you may be used to having to speak loudly to make yourself heard. When talking to someone who grew up under similar circumstances and shares your style of communication, you may find that you get on like a house on fire. However, when trying to converse with someone who is a lot more reserved, you may find it difficult to find common ground and carry a conversation. Conversely, while you may choose to loudly vocalize your feelings, this style of communication may be off-putting and even scary for someone with a different style of communication. You may be alienating people without even realizing that your behavior is impacting them negatively.

Communicating while angry is even more difficult than normal communication. For many reasons, it can be difficult to effectively communicate with someone who has made you angry. This difficulty can be increased if the person that you are trying to communicate with is also angry. However, in order to express your anger in a way that does not damage your relationships with others, it is important to learn and understand methods for adjusting your communication style and communicating effectively when you're angry.

COMMUNICATING WHEN ANGRY

A lot of the damage done by anger is either increased or directly caused by a breakdown in communication. Increased levels of cortisol inhibits activity in the prefrontal cortex of our brains, which affects our ability to make good decisions and choose our words carefully. On top of this, the fight or flight instinct results in the automatic response of raising our voices, which tends to only escalate arguments. The combination of these two natural reactions to anger results in vocal expressions that are both poorly worded and aggressive in tone. The person on the receiving end of such a response may be triggered and respond in kind, thus creating a vicious cycle of angry communication, which more often than not yields unproductive and/or mutually detrimental results.

AGGRESSIVE VERSUS ASSERTIVE

While it is definitely important to express your anger, there is a fine line between aggressive expressions of anger and assertive expressions of anger.

Assertive communication is a way to effectively convey your wants, needs, and feelings to other people. It is a means to achieve a desired result without causing harm to the people around you or your relationships with them. It does not necessarily mean beating around the bush or keeping things to yourself, rather being honest yet tactful—choosing your words and timing carefully.

Aggressive communication is more reactive than reflective. It lacks planning and aforethought and relies on the raw emotion of anger to craft sentences. This type of communication is the path to further conflict. Because of the lack of thought behind words of aggression, you are often prone to say things that you don't actually mean, making the communication less honest than if you were to take a moment to gather truer thoughts.

Being adept in assertive communication can lead to extremely positive outcomes, not just for yourself but also for the people you are at odds with. It can help you express your anger in terms that can be clearly understood, which helps the other party or parties understand where you're coming from. This leads to a more collaborative style of communication, rather than the combative style that follows aggressive communication. By utilizing assertive communication, you can facilitate empathy on both sides and work together toward a mutually beneficial solution.

Your ability to utilize assertive communication will depend on a number of factors. First, you will need to develop your self-awareness and self-regulation, so that you are able to recognize when you are angry and stop yourself from reflexively saying the first thought that pops into your head. Second, you will need to remain silent for long enough to gather your thoughts and rehearse your response, even if this means walking away for now and returning once you have been able to get your thoughts in order. Finally, you will need exercise empathy, to see not only the other side's point of view, but also decide on the best style of communication with which to convey your feelings to them. Remember that different people will respond better to different styles of communication. Try to think about the other person's personality, your previous experience with them as a person, and choose a method of communication that they are likely to respond positively to.

A DOWNWARD SPIRAL

Anger is one of many emotions associated with hostility. As explained in the previous chapter, anger can trigger or be triggered by a range of other negative emotions, causing a downward spiral of negativity that is sure to cause communication to break down. It is important to be aware of these other negative emotions, so that you can recognize that they are an expression of your anger and ensure that they do not cause you to victimize the person with whom you are trying to communicate.

Contempt is an offshoot of anger and it can make you feel that you are better than someone else. This feeling may lead you to insult or mock the other person, belittling them and making fun of them. These kinds of expressions, even if you feel that they are done in jest, send negative messages to the other person; messages such as judgment, disapproval, and disrespect. This creates a cycle of negativity within the relationship. Often in these types of contemptuous relationships, one party will cause the other to withdraw and become distant, leading to conflict becoming unresolved.

Disgust can also be a secondary emotion to anger and will cause you to reject or avoid the source of your disgust. You may feel disgust with a person if their values, beliefs, or behaviors cause you intense feelings of hatred or disapproval. This will motivate you to avoid them and even people or locations associated with them. However, it is important to try to understand differing points of view, even if you cannot fully agree with them.

Jealousy can also occur when angry and is actually a combination of emotions. We feel jealous when we feel that we are at risk of losing something of value because of another person. The emotions that cause jealousy are fear of the loss of something precious, anger at the person that is threatening to take it from us, and sadness at the prospect of losing it. Envy is similar, but not to be confused with jealousy. Envy is caused by our desire for something that another person possesses.

Sadness and anxiousness can also be caused by anger. However, this type of emotion is more likely to motivate us to withdraw rather than attack. While this may seem less destructive to relationships, it can be just as damaging as it prevents effective communication from even being attempted.

All of the negative emotions associated with anger hinder positive communication. An awareness of these emotions and the drive and strategy to overcome them and express them is the key to preventing them from damaging your relationships.

FACILITATING POSITIVE COMMUNICATION

In order to ensure that your anger does not lead to a cycle of negativity and poor communication, you need to learn how to break that cycle and how to facilitate positive communication and constructive expressions of anger. If you can master this, you will be able to maintain positive relationships while making sure that your feelings are expressed and your needs are being met.

THINK BEFORE YOU SPEAK

This is crucial in facilitating positive communication. When you're angered, saying the first thing that comes to mind will only seek to cause harm to your target. The harm inflicted on them will most likely cause them to strike back in kind, thus beginning the vicious cycle.

Thinking before you speak will require you to stop yourself in the heat of the moment and pause long enough to gather your thoughts. Learn to stay silent. If the other person is venting, learn to actively listen to them, even if their words are making you angry. Use your increased understanding of anger to recognize the anger that is driving *their* actions. Angry people often just need to vent and if you take the time to silently listen to their complaints, they will often calm down on their own. Communication is a two-way street. If you're both trying to talk over each other without really listening to what the other is saying, you're going to get nowhere.

Once you have heard their side of the argument, think about their words. Ask yourself honestly if their complaints are valid. Try looking at the situation from their point of view. If it helps, step outside of your own metaphorical shoes and imagine putting yourself in theirs.

As an example, let's consider the following scenario. You've returned home after a long and gruelling day of work and found that the front door to your house is wide open. Panicked that something terrible has happened, you rush inside to find your partner in the kitchen busy with the stove. You ask them why the front door was open and they tell you that they must have left it open by mistake when they came home from the supermarket. You begin telling your partner off for being so careless, and remind them that the area you live in is not the safest area and that just two days ago the apartment two doors down from you was broken into. Your partner gets upset at your tone and an argument between the two of you ensues.

The anger that you feel in response to this situation comes from a place that means well. You are aware of the danger of leaving the door open and you were worried that something had happened to your partner. You don't wish for your partner to come to any harm so you want to remind them to be more careful about home security.

Now, let's step into your partner's shoes and look at the events that led up to the argument from their perspective. Your partner understands that you work hard and wants to reward you by preparing a nice dinner for the two of you.

Despite having a heavy schedule themselves and not being a huge fan of cooking, they've looked up a recipe for your favorite meal and gone to the supermarket to purchase the ingredients for said meal. The ingredients are heavy and they need to be carried in both hands, but your partner manages to lug the groceries up four flights of stairs, unlock the door somehow, and get the groceries into the apartment. Since their hands are full, they decide to drop the groceries off in the kitchen before coming back to close the door. However, the thoughts of preparing the meal distract them and they inevitably forget to close the door. They understand the importance of locking the door and this is the first time they've ever made this mistake.

Forgetting about the door, they begin to get busy in the kitchen preparing your favorite meal. Cooking the meal is stressful for them as they are not much of a cook, but after slaving away at a hot stove for two hours, they manage to prepare the meal and are pleasantly surprised with how well it turned out. When you arrive home, they expect to receive gratitude for the delicious smells emanating from the kitchen. Instead, you talk about the front door and begin accosting them, not even noticing the delicious meal that they have spent hours preparing.

Every situation has multiple ways of looking at it. If you're only prepared to consider your side, your view of the world will become very narrow. By taking the time to exercise empathy and think about the point of view of others, you can give yourself a broader outlook and put yourself in a position better suited to gauging the objective truth of the situation. If you are lucky enough, your partner will be able to rationally explain their point of view to you, but don't rely on this. Listen to their words, understand their situation, and read in between the lines of what they are saying.. Then ask yourself how you can best respond to their complaints.

Once you have considered the other person's point of view, it's time to articulate your own point of view. Take the time to craft your response and choose your words carefully. If you have to, walk away from the conversation and take the time to rehearse a response. This may be time consuming, but it is crucial to ensuring that the other person will receive your feelings clearly and better understand where you're coming from. An added benefit of this is that the time between your initial argument and your rehearsed response will give you both time to cool down.

STICK WITH "I" STATEMENTS

Assigning blame is always detrimental to communication. When people feel they are being blamed, they become defensive and less open to honest communication.

In order to avoid this, try sticking to "I" statements. "An 'I' statement is a form of communication that focuses on the feelings or beliefs of the speaker rather than thoughts and characteristics that the speaker attributes to the listener" (Good Therapy, 2019). For example, the question, "Why do you never help out around the house?" places the blame on the listener, making them feel attacked. However, the explanation of, "I feel overwhelmed and unappreciated when I am left to do all the household chores," explains to the listener how the speaker is feeling as a result of the current situation.

When used correctly, an "I" statement can help a person become aware of problematic behavior without laying the blame solely on one party. It motivates both parties to take responsibility for their own thoughts and actions, rather than attributing to one another.

This technique is often used during professional counselling sessions. During these sessions, the counsellor can guide the parties involved in the correct use of "I" statements, since not all "I" statements are effective ways of expressing feelings. For example, the statement, "I hate it when you don't help me out around the house," technically does start with an "I," but it is not the healthiest form of expression.

Here are some examples of the correct use of "I" statements compared to their equivalent "you" statement:

Scenario 1: You are angry at your teammate for making many mistakes. A common "you" statement would be, "Get your head in the game!" A more effective "I" statement would be, "I'm feeling disappointed at the prospect of losing this game."

Scenario 2: You received the incorrect order at a restaurant and are angry with the server. A common "you" statement would be, "You need to give me a refund." A more effective "I" statement would be, "I feel unsatisfied with the level of service I've experienced."

Scenario 3: You failed to receive a promotion at work and are angry with your boss. A common "you" statement would be, "You don't appreciate the work that I do." A more effective "I" statement would be, "I feel that I am qualified and have worked hard for this promotion, so I am confused as to why I was overlooked."

USE HUMOR

Humor can be an effective tool in disarming tension. However, it is important not to confuse mockery with humor. While mockery seeks to make fun of a person and belittle them, constructive humor doesn't have a target and instead gives everybody something to laugh about.

In order to use humor to effectively diffuse a situation, try analyzing the situation and finding the lighter side of it. Once you have succeeded in finding the lighter side of it, make a comment that does not intend to cause harm but rather make the other side laugh. The comment doesn't even have to be particularly funny. People rarely *want* to feel angry. More often than not, anger is a defensive response to a perceived threat. If you respond to a person's anger with untargeted levity, it will show the person that you are not looking for a fight. This will make them feel less defensive and less trapped, providing them with an out if they do not wish to continue an argument. Halting the argument in its tracks will cause an enormous sense of relief in both parties, resulting in both of you calming down long enough to hold a constructive conversation.

If you are unable to come up with a witticism for the situation, try simply smiling or laughing. Not a creepy, maniacal, Joker-esque laugh, but rather a subtle and serene smile or chuckle. Doing this will send similar signals of peace to the person you are arguing with, letting them know that you don't wish to fight. It also has the added benefit of boosting your own mood and calming you down.

USE POSITIVE BODY LANGUAGE

In today's age of digital communication, it can be difficult to keep in mind the added complexities of face-to-face communication. One such complexity is body language.

Body language can tell you a lot about a person and vice versa. It's something that we don't have to worry about when we are texting or emailing, so it can be something that is easily forgotten when talking to someone in person. Slumped shoulders, downcast eyes, and folded arms might seem harmless, but these kinds of actions can convey dishonesty or lack of self-confidence. You may not even be conscious of performing these actions, yet the person you are talking to is sure to notice them.

When it comes to anger, there are a number of automatic bodily reactions that will clearly communicate to a person that you are angry. Some of these have been discussed in previous chapters of this book; things like pacing back and forth, clenching your hands into fists, and frowning. Even subtle changes in your manner like a widening in your stance, leaning in a tad too closely, or clenching your jaw can be seen as subtle acts of aggression.

When trying to communicate with someone effectively, it is important to be mindful of your body language and adjust your mannerisms with movements that will succeed in building trust between yourself and the person you are talking to.

Instead of clenching your fists, use open palm gestures. "Open palms are a sign of peaceful intentions. It shows that you have nothing to hide, you're unarmed, and you're mentally open to what the other person is saying" (Umoh, 2018). When someone talks to you and gestures with their palms open rather than closed, they are easier to trust. Once trust is shared between both parties, communication becomes easier.

Maintaining eye contact is also a good way to build trust. People who avert their gaze too readily come across as dishonest or insincere. However, too much eye contact can come across as aggressive or threatening. A good rule of thumb when conversing with someone is to look them in the eye for 70% of the time. This will show the person that you are interested in hearing them out without coming across as too intense.

Tilting your head can show someone that you are willing to adopt a more vulnerable position. With the simple action of showing our neck to the person we are speaking to, you can convey to them that you are ready to listen to their side. This will allow them to open up to you without fear and they will be less likely to feel hostility toward you.

Be sure to keep your arms uncrossed when speaking to people and face them straight on, rather than angling your body away from them. Crossed arms send the signal that you do not particularly wish to communicate and have already made up your mind. Similarly, failing to face the person directly tells them that you have no interest in the conversation and that you are ready to leave.

Body language plays a huge part in face-to-face communication. However, it is not something that is universal for all cultures. For example, in Western culture maintaining eye contact is a sign of respect, but in Asia it can be a sign of insubordination. When in doubt, try to mirror other people's body language or adopt a softer stance than you normally would. Be mindful of your facial expression as this is often the first thing people see. A frown conveys anger no matter who you're talking to.

PUT IT IN WRITING

If you become so angry that you find articulating yourself very difficult, try writing down your feelings. Go away and write a letter to the person you are angry with. Get all of your feelings down on the page and hold onto the letter for a few days. Once a few days have passed and you have calmed down, read the letter through and compare your current thoughts with the thoughts that you put down on paper.

Writing down your feelings can be just as cathartic as expressing them verbally or physically. Writing also involves a lot of time and thought, two things that are beneficial in alleviating anger. The act of writing can cause you to calm down, so much so that you may not even feel the need to finish the letter.

Reading the letter once some time has passed will allow you to reexamine your anger with some objectivity. Reading the words on a page will create a separation between yourself at the moment of reading and the feelings you were experiencing at the moment that triggered your anger. It will almost be like you are reading a story that has happened to someone else. The objectivity caused by this effect will allow you to be more honest about whether your anger was justified. It will also allow you to take a more deliberate approach to expressing your anger. You will be able to see words and phrases that are potentially harmful to your relationship with the other person and readjust them in order to prevent harm.

Chapter 6:
Preparing for Anger

Anger is an inevitability of life. You are just as likely to eliminate the need for anger as you are to eliminate the need for oxygen. There are always going to be situations in life that are bound to cause anger. There is no point trying to avoid it or trying to avoid having to deal with it.

Being prepared for anger is the best way to keep it under control. Just like with anything in life, preparation will make you more likely to achieve the desired results. If you prepare yourself with the tools and techniques that have proven to be effective in controlling your anger and you have developed your ability to recognize the warning signs of your anger, you will be better equipped to deal with the inevitability of the emotion.

IF YOU WANT PEACE, PREPARE FOR WAR

So how do you prepare for anger? Well, how do you prepare for anything? How would someone prepare for climbing Mount Everest? They would need to prepare their mind for the arduous challenge, learning everything about the mountain itself and the life-saving techniques that will help them scale it. They would need to prepare their body for the challenge, getting themselves into peak physical condition. They would also need to prepare the tools they require for the journey to ensure that once they are on the mountain, they are equipped with everything they need.

For some people, controlling their anger can be a challenge akin to climbing Mount Everest. However difficult you feel controlling your anger may be, just like climbing Everest, it is not impossible. Provided, you are sufficiently prepared.

You have taken the first step toward preparing yourself for anger. You have committed yourself to learning more about your anger and the techniques that can be used to control it. In the next section, we will talk about the tools that you can equip yourself with as well as the physical conditioning that you can undergo in order to overcome the seemingly insurmountable peak of your anger.

HEALTHY BODY, HEALTHY MIND

It may seem like a cliche but a healthy body does usually lead to a healthy mind. Maintaining healthy habits and avoiding unhealthy habits is a crucial element in making sure that your anger is controllable.

First of all, make sure that you get plenty of sleep. "A large body of research supports the connection between sleep deprivation and mood changes such as increased anger and aggression" (Saghir et al., 2018). One such study was performed by Iowa State University in which 142 participants were divided into two groups. The first group maintained their regular sleep routine, an average of about seven hours a night. The second group cut their sleep short by two to four hours each night over two nights, averaging at around four and a half hours of sleep a night. After the second night, both groups were subjected to sounds designed to make the participants feel uncomfortable. Predictably, the group that had been sleep restricted reported more anger and aggression in response to the noises.

The typical person needs seven to eight hours of sleep each night to maintain peak physical and mental health. Anything less than this is referred to as sleep deprivation and can be harmful to your health. Consecutive nights of sleep deprivation can result in what is known as sleep debt. Sleep debt reduces the brain's ability to suppress activity in the amygdala. This results in emotional instability and an increased tendency toward emotions such as anger. A tired person will be less able to control their emotional state than a person who has been able to have a good amount of sleep.

Another important part of making sure to keep healthy enough to keep anger at bay is to avoid substances that can contribute to anger. These substances include, but are not limited to, narcotics and alcohol, which are often associated with increased aggression and violence. In fact, a research article published by the Association of Psychological Science states that alcohol is a contributor to about half of all violent crimes committed in the US, including rape, murder, spousal and child abuse, and assault.

In the short-term, alcohol affects the judgment center of the brain, lowering inhibitions and impulse control. This can lead to poor social judgment and may in fact create situations that cause other people anger. On top of this, alcohol raises a person's blood pressure and can cause mood swings and irritability, making controlling anger and other emotions difficult. This is why it is not unusual for a physical fight to break out between two drunk individuals and also why these individuals may be hugging each other mere hours later.

A particular danger of drugs and alcohol for angry individuals is that they can act as a crutch. Substances such as these can be used to numb pain and can be relied on too heavily to quell angry thoughts, rather than dealing with them on an emotional level. This behavior often leads to substance abuse, where angry thoughts will spark cravings for drugs or alcohol, the use of which can spark feelings of pain and anguish, thus creating a cycle of dependence. If you are an angry person, it may be best to avoid drinking alcohol altogether.

One more key component in keeping healthy is exercise. Exercise is cathartic and is good for releasing energy created by pent up feelings of aggression. By finding the right form of physical activity, you can release this energy in a way that not only ensures there are no casualties to your anger (unless you count the punching bag), but also improves your physical condition. Keeping in good physical condition will help maintain your mood, regulate your blood pressure, and promote clear thought processes.

BREATHING EXERCISES

We've mentioned previously the benefits of counting down from 10 when you are angry. This technique is further enhanced by implementing specific breathing techniques in between each count. By concentrating on slow, controlled breathing, you distract your mind by focusing on your breathing rather than your anger. Also, the conscious act of slowing down your breathing will help tell your brain that you are not in danger and help settle your nerves. In order to be prepared for anger, learn and memorize a variety of breathing exercises so that you can start doing them as soon as you start to feel angry, as well as afterwards to continuously manage your anger once you have some time to yourself.

As soon as you sense yourself getting angry, begin counting down from 10. At the same time, start focusing on controlling your breathing. Focus on breathing from your diaphragm rather than your chest and try to relax your face and muscles as you breathe. Breathe in deeply through your nose and feel your belly expand with the breath. Envision yourself drawing the air into your stomach. If it helps you concentrate, close your eyes and place your hands over your belly as you breathe. Hold the breath for a moment, count the first number, then exhale deeply through your mouth, feeling your belly flatten. Continue this pattern of breathing until you have counted all the way down to zero. If you still feel angry at that point, start the count again.

Another breathing technique that you can practice is the 4-7-8 breathing technique by Dr. Andrew Weil. This technique involves the same kind of breathing, that is from the diaphragm rather than the chest, but it implements a specific count to help distract the mind and promote relaxation. As you're inhaling count slowly to four, hold your breath and continue the count to seven, then exhale while continuing to count to eight. Repeat this pattern of counts until you feel yourself calming down.

These techniques can be used to immediately diffuse anger, but it is also important to practice them when you aren't feeling stressed or angry. Practicing will help build the skill for later use and make it an automatic response to anger. Performing the activity in a peaceful setting will also allow you to associate the act of deep breathing with peace and tranquility. When you have free time, find a quiet and comfortable place to practice your breathing exercises. If you can, try to practice several times a day. You can even try relaxing workouts that incorporate breathing exercises, such as yoga or Tai Chi.

PROGRESSIVE MUSCLE RELAXATION

Progressive muscle relaxation (PMR) is an anxiety-reducing technique that dates back all the way to the 1930s. The technique involves alternating tension and relaxation in all of the body's major muscle groups. As discussed in earlier chapters, anger can cause the involuntary tensing of muscles. Learning how to relax these muscles by using PMR will give you a valuable tool for controlling your anger.

In order to perform PMR, first find a quiet place where you can relax and lie down. Try to wear non-restrictive clothing and remove any accessories such as eye glasses or jewelry. Place your hands in your lap or by your sides and exercise controlled breathing, as discussed in the previous section.

Now, focus your attention on the following areas in order, making sure to keep the rest of your body in a relaxed state. Do not use your hands or other parts of your body to engage each muscle group, but rather activate the individual muscles independently. As you're activating and deactivating each muscle group, remember to continue your deep, even breathing.

First, squeeze the muscles in your forehead by frowning or grimacing. Hold for 15 seconds and feel the muscles become tighter and tenser. Then, slowly release the tension in your forehead while counting for 30 seconds. Continue to release the tension until your forehead becomes completely relaxed.

Next, tense the muscles in your jaw. Again, hold for 15 seconds before releasing the tension over 30 seconds. Be sure to notice the feeling of relaxation as you ease the tension.

Next, increase the tension in your neck and shoulders by raising your shoulders toward your ears. Hold this position for 15 seconds, then slowly lower your shoulders and release the tension over 30 seconds.

Next, slowly curl your hands into fists and pull your fists to your chest, squeezing as tight as you can. Hold this position for 15 seconds before slowly releasing the tension over 30 seconds.

Next, slowly tense your buttocks over 15 seconds until you are clenching as tight as you can. Release the tension over 30 seconds and feel yourself relaxing.

Next, slowly increase the tension in your quadriceps and calves over 15 seconds. Squeeze the muscles as hard as you can, then release the tension over 30 seconds.

Finally, slowly increase the tension in your feet and toes by curling your toes into fists over 15 seconds. Tighten the muscles as much as you can, then slowly release the tension over 30 seconds.

This exercise, in conjunction with deep breathing exercises, has been proven to relax feelings of anxiety and anger. Again, practice makes perfect. Try to practice as much as you can, even when you are feeling relatively at ease. In order to make the steps easier to remember, try recording or downloading a set of audio prompts onto your phone, so that you can play the track as you're practicing.

MUSIC TO SOOTHE THE SAVAGE BEAST

There are many ways in which music can aid in anger management. The right piece of music for the right moment can be a powerful tool for controlling your emotional state. For this reason, a proven method for anger management exists in the form of "music therapy."

The first goal of music therapy is to help you get a better gauge of your stress level. This has to do with developing your emotional awareness. By analyzing and discussing songs that tell stories, you can personalize the situation and examine how you would feel if you found yourself in the same situation. Listen to a rap song by notoriously angry rapper Eminem and try to objectively predict how you would feel if you were in his shoes. By utilizing this technique with songs that tell different stories, you will be able to exercise empathy while developing a better sense of your own emotional response. You can also analyze the tone of the songs to gain an understanding of how the artist expresses their anger and in doing so, get a better sense of your comparative response to anger, whether it be passive, assertive, or aggressive. The music of Alanis Morisette is very different to the music of Eminem. Both have produced songs from a place of anger, but the anger is expressed in different ways. Experiment with different styles and genres and experience a range of different expressions of anger.

Aside from discussing music as a means to explore your emotions compared to those of the artists that wrote the songs, the music itself can be a source of catharsis and/or relaxation. It's important to note that because of differences in musical taste, the music genre and style that is most effective in calming you down will not be universal for everyone. Some people may find that listening to heavy metal allows them to vent their anger. Others may find that classical music helps them relax and focus their mind. Others still may find that listening to comical music stylings, such as parody songs by "Weird Al" Yankovic, can make them feel better by making them laugh.

Try exploring different types of music, both as an exploration of emotion and as a means to discover the music that best helps you to relax. Experiment with different types of music and once you find what works for you, make sure to have a lot of it cued up on your iPod and ready to go once you start to feel angry.

It should be said that the act of playing music can also be cathartic, particularly if it involves physical exertion like drumming. Japanese students and workers have been known to frequent karaoke establishments on their own, so that they can belt out their favorite tunes in a private release of their pent up anger or stress. Don't be shy. Give it a go. Not only might you find the act of singing or playing music therapeutic, but you might discover that you are actually a talented musician.

FIND YOUR HAPPY PLACE

Finding your "happy place" involves positive visualization and combines the method of distraction with a temporary escape from a stressful situation. When you start to feel yourself getting angry, close your eyes, start breathing, and focus on visualizing your happy place. See it in your mind's eye, think about what it sounds like, what it smells like, and what the air feels like. Doing this will allow all feelings of anger and anxiety to melt away.

It may be tough for you to find your happy place, as it is different for each person. It should be a place that relaxes you and calms you down, but it should also be a place that you know quite well so that you can recall specific details about it on command and fully immerse yourself in the calming environment. For some people, their happy place may be a babbling brook that ran by the house they grew up in. For others, it might be a busy shopping mall on the first Christmas Eve they remember.

Here are some tips to finding your happy place.

First of all, ask yourself who or what makes you happy. Is it spending time with your family or friends or is it spending time in quiet solitude? Is it exercising, travelling, or doing something you're passionate about?

Next, recall a place or point in time where you were able to experience deep contentment. Remember where you were, who you were with, and what you were doing. Remember the scenery. Was it outdoors or indoors? Perhaps you were at the beach. Perhaps you were at your grandparents' house. Remember the sounds that you heard. The laughing of your children. The sounds of the waves caressing the shore. The distant calling of birds.

Commit specific details of your happy place to memory. This will make your happy place feel more real and will allow you to get lost in the memory. If your happy place happens to be somewhere that you can physically travel to, go there and take some time to savor the moment and memorize the feeling of being there. If you happen to have an experience that causes you great happiness, document it. Write it down as soon as it happens to you in great detail, so that it will be easier to recall when needed.

Finding your happy place will give you the freedom to lose yourself in the moment. With the right state of mind, going to your happy place will become easier and easier.

THE CALM-DOWN KIT

Though the calm-down kit was originally used by parents wanting to calm down anxious kids, it is actually a valuable tool for controlling anger in adults as well. We all have items that calm us down. Usually they are items that we associate with positive thoughts or experiences. Try to isolate these items and keep them in a literal box that you can access whenever you feel uncontrollably angry. The items should be small enough to hold in your hand and provide you with a range of stimuli to engage your five senses.

The first item should be something that calms you down just by looking at it, for example, a photograph of a fond memory or a DVD of your favorite movie. The second item should be something that is pleasant to touch, hold, or manipulate in your hands. This could be a fidget spinner, a childhood toy, or a stress ball. The third item should be something that smells nice or comforting, like some potpourri or a scented candle. The fourth item should be something that engages your ears and provides a soothing sound. This could be a recording of your favorite song or podcast. The last item should be a non-perishable food item that, when you taste it, allows you to recall a happier time. A good example of this is a type of gum or candy that you used to enjoy as a kid.

Once you have assembled your calm-down kit, you can use it as a last resort to controlling your anger. If you utilize a range of anger management techniques, you will rarely feel the need to go for your calm-down kit. Often, the mere act of thinking about your calm-down kit will be enough to calm you down and the fact that your calm-down kit exists will provide comfort in and of itself.

Chapter 7:
Living With Anger

Anger has consequences on your mind, body, and relationships. Dealing with the consequences of your anger in a healthy way is important in managing your anger. Recognize that nobody is perfect. Try as you might to control your anger, there may be times when anger gets the better of you and you may end up doing something that you regret, causing damage to yourself or the people around you. That's okay. Mistakes happen and can be fixed, as long as you are willing to try.

REPAIRING BONDS

Even at the best of times, maintaining healthy relationships with everyone that we care about can be difficult. If you are prone to anger, this task is compounded exponentially. Even if you are equipped with all the anger management techniques available, there is still a chance that you may say something or do something in anger that hurts someone. While the damage caused by these hurtful actions may seem irredeemable and you may feel extreme guilt and shame once you've calmed down, it's important to remember that most relationships are worth salvaging. Even if it seems hopeless, you have to at least try to fix the damage that you've inadvertently caused.

WRITE A LETTER

As previously discussed, putting your feelings down on paper is a great way to articulate your thoughts in a tactful and well-thought out way. It is a far better expression of emotion than words said in anger in the midst of an argument.

Writing down your feelings will also allow you to reflect upon your own actions and emotions. As you write you will feel the burden on your shoulders ease with each word and you will allow yourself to let go of all that negative energy, even if the intended reader of your letter never even looks at it.

An added benefit to writing a letter is that it puts the onus on the recipient to read it. You may have hurt them so deeply that time is needed for them to even think about forgiving you. That's fine. They can read the letter whenever they feel ready to. The beauty of a letter is that the words and feelings expressed within them remain unchanged no matter how much time passes.

SAY "NO" TO GRUDGES

Forgiveness goes both ways. It's just as important to forgive people that have caused you anger as it is to seek forgiveness from people you have wronged. For this reason, it is important to refrain from holding grudges against people that you feel have wronged you.

Holding grudges can negatively impact your relationships in a variety of ways. Essentially a grudge is unresolved anger in a relationship, the result of anger that has not been processed and resolved properly. This leads to feelings of resentment on one or both sides of the relationship. If you continue to hold a grudge against someone, not only will you feel resentment toward this person, but this person will also begin to resent you for being unable to let go. These feelings of resentment fester over time, gradually turning into bitterness. Once it reaches this point, it is extremely difficult to repair the bond.

If you find yourself holding a grudge against someone, it is important to reflect on your anger and ask yourself why you are continuing to hold the grudge. If the grudge was caused by the actions of the person you are angry with, it's important to communicate this to them clearly, so that they can be made aware of their actions and your resultant feelings. Once they are aware, it is up to them how they want to address the issue, but at least the issue will be addressed, for better or for worse.

Talk to the people that make you angry, even if the offense seems petty and slight. Let them know how you're feeling. No good can come from holding onto your anger in the form of a grudge. Doing so will create a habit of grudge-holding that will make it difficult for you to maintain healthy relationships.

If you are not emotionally ready to forgive someone, try to simply imagine forgiving them. Imagine sitting across from them and saying those words: "I forgive you." Imagine how saying that sentence would make you feel. Imagine how hearing that sentence would make them feel. You may find your anger slipping away just by pretending that you're forgiving them.

THE RIGHT WAY TO EXPRESS ANGER

We've established that expressing anger the wrong way can be destructive to your relationships, but how do you express anger the right way?

This involves putting everything we've talked about in previous chapters together. First, you need to understand your anger and be able to identify it when it occurs. Then, you need to take the time to implement anger management strategies that can be used to calm yourself down. You will only be able to express your anger in a constructive and healthy manner if you are doing so from a position of calm and reason. Once you have calmed yourself, you will need to gather your thoughts, think about the person with whom you're trying to communicate, and articulate yourself in a manner that is not going to cause harm.

Avoid passive-aggressive expressions of anger and actually deal directly with the person who angered you. Avoid expressing yourself aggressively by raising your voice. Instead, cultivate a mutual respect by expressing yourself assertively. Avoid laying blame and use "I" statements to simply raise the facts—facts pertaining to the situation and your feelings regarding the situation. Identify the specific emotions that you felt and clearly lay them out for the other person. Try to be specific when talking about your emotions, rather than saying that you felt "good" or "bad." Give specific examples of what made you feel a particular way, for example, "I feel jealous when I see you spending more time with your friends than me."

Be sure to be respectful of the other person and use polite phrasing and expressions, such as "please" and "thank you." Finally, focus on problem solving rather than problem stating. Look past the initial trigger of your anger and look toward solutions to the problems that have arisen because of the situation. Once you can do this, you'll be able to cooperate with the person that has angered you and vice versa. Both of you will be able to work together toward a mutually beneficial outcome.

Positive assertive communication can be difficult to achieve and will take time to master. However, if you are able to communicate your frustrations clearly, concisely, and politely, you will be much better equipped to maintain relationships despite your anger.

FINDING THE RIGHT OUTLET

Living with anger will necessitate a means to vent your anger; to release the pent up energy caused by the body's response to anger. Anger gives you a surge of energy and can be a powerful motivator toward positive change, provided you have a positive outlet for this energy.

Finding the right outlet for you to channel your angry energy toward is a matter of identifying your priorities and interests, then experimenting with different avenues that explore these interests.

EXERCISE

The health benefits of exercise are obvious and well-documented. However, exercise is also a viable means to regulate feelings of anger, making exercise not only important for your physical wellbeing, but also your mental wellbeing.

Almost all forms of exercise can succeed in reducing anger levels, as all exercise uses up energy, whether it be healthy energy or angry energy. The difficulty comes in choosing the right form of exercise for you. While you may acknowledge that a particular form of exercise is effective in managing your anger, this may not be enough of a motivator to continue with an exercise regime. For example, if you find running boring you may not want to continue doing it even if it is reducing your blood pressure. In fact, the fact that it bores you may cause you to become irritated at the thought of going out for a run.

Luckily, there are a huge number of exercises to choose from. Have some fun exploring your options and finding the exercise that resonates with you; something you enjoy doing so much that you don't even think of it as a means for regulating your anger but rather an enjoyable hobby that you look forward to doing. Here are some ideas to get you started.

Take a boxing or kickboxing class to release the anger that you're holding onto. Rather than taking out your anger on a person, you can take it out on a punching bag. These sports are not only great for releasing stress, they are excellent cardio workouts.

Walking is a physical activity that not only lowers stress hormones but also provides time for self-reflection. By going out for a brisk walk, you provide yourself with a change of scenery and with it a change in perspective. You allow yourself to be alone with your thoughts while giving yourself a workout.

Studies show that weight lifting and strength training are linked to reduced anxiety and increased self-awareness. As you become stronger, you will also gain self-confidence, which will allow you to communicate with others in a more assertive way.

Joining a team sport can help you practice teamwork and cooperation. You will learn to work well with others toward a shared goal. You will also learn to focus and be able to release mental stress on the field. Be advised that competitive sport may not be a viable choice for regulating anger for everyone, so maybe stick to friendly matches instead, where the stakes are lower.

Skipping rope, jogging, or cycling are all forms of aerobic exercise that can get your heart pumping and ease feelings of anxiety and anger. Because of their rhythmic and repetitive nature, they are great for regulating breathing and strong emotions.

Spiritual exercises like yoga and Tai Chi combine muscle relaxation techniques with deep breathing exercises. This combination of elements, when paired with a spiritual approach, make these kinds of exercises particularly effective in clearing the mind and washing away all feelings of anger.

CREATIVITY

If exercise is not your cup of tea or health issues prevent you from undergoing rigorous training regimens, perhaps a more creative avenue of anger expression would be more suitable for you.

Anger is a passionate emotion. This passion can be expressed in works of art across a variety of platforms, whether it be through music, paint, sculpture, or creative writing. Expressing your anger through creative works not only provides you with an outlet for your anger, but it also provides you with an insight into your innermost feelings. If you tap into your rage to create a painting, this painting is a visual representation of what you're feeling. Examining it will be like looking through a window into your very soul and may reveal something about yourself that you previously were unaware of.

What is necessary for utilizing anger in creative endeavors is first your willingness to accept your anger and face your darkest thoughts. Rather than ignoring that darkness or hiding it, you will need to embrace it. By actively seeking out your anger in order to utilize it in your art, you will open a doorway to wisdom and creativity, while at the same time dealing with your emotions in a healthy way.

By welcoming this anger you will strip it of its destructive power. Rather than a force that seeks to destroy your life, it will become a partner in your creative endeavors. You will be able to release the full power of your anger onto the canvas, or the page, or whatever medium you choose. This will result in honest and powerful works of art, as well as a clearer mind and healthier expression of emotion.

MEDITATION

Much like the recitation of a mantra, the act of meditation is not about controlling anger or suppressing it, but rather controlling how we react to it. Consistent use of meditation can help increase your emotional intelligence and allow you to feel the emotion and let it pass without holding onto it or responding to it the wrong way. It can also be used as a tool to calm down when you are angry or enraged, since it involves deep breathing and relaxation of the body and mind.

Meditation is an ancient tradition that is still practiced in cultures all over the world as a means to create a sense of calm and inner harmony. Yet despite its history and popularity, there are many barriers to actually trying it out. For a beginner, the process of meditation can be a bit daunting. For the skeptic, meditation may even seem a bit silly. However you may feel about meditation, it has been proven to provide benefits such as reducing stress, promoting emotional health, and enhancing self-awareness. It is also quite easy to do, once you've gotten the hang of it.

There are several types of meditation and it may take some experimentation to find the style of meditation that is most suitable for you.

Spiritual meditation is used in Eastern religions and is similar to prayer in that you utilize silence to reflect on the universe and seek a closer connection to a higher power. Spiritual meditation can be practiced at home or in a place of worship and are often aided by the use of essential oils such as frankincense, myrrh, sage, cedar, and sandalwood.

Focused meditation involves concentration on any one of your five senses. This style of meditation does not encourage letting your mind wander, as do other styles of meditation, but instead requires you to focus your attention on something audible, visual, or physical. For example, people who practice focused meditation often do so by counting mala beads in their hand, focusing on the weight and number of the beads. Others practice focused meditation by listening to the sound of a gong, focusing on the sound resonating in the space around them. Another option is to stare at the flame of a candle, focusing on the flickering of its light. Whatever item you use to aid in focused meditation, it is important that you bring your focus back to the object if you begin to sense your mind wandering.

Movement meditation combines meditation with gentle movements. This form of meditation is synonymous with yoga, but the movement involved can be as simple as a gentle stroll through peaceful surroundings, such as a garden or a forest. It could even be practiced by doing something practical yet therapeutic such as gardening or knitting. Whatever action you utilize for movement meditation, it is important that it is a gentle and peaceful movement, nothing too dynamic.

Mantra meditation involves the repetitive chanting of a sound, word, or phrase. By focusing on the sound, you will become more alert and in tune with your environment. The sound used for mantra meditation can be any sound that brings you relaxation and it can be spoken at any volume and pace you choose, though a slow pace is usually more relaxing.

Mindfulness meditation originates from Buddhist teachings and is the most popular meditation technique in the West. It involves paying attention to the thoughts and feelings that pass through your mind at various stages of the meditation process, simply acknowledging them and taking note of their patterns. This type of meditation is easy to do on your own. Though it does not usually require a teacher, when first getting started you may find that sitting still and doing nothing is surprisingly difficult. Since this type of meditation is most practical for home use, the following section will break down the steps for mindfulness meditation.

In order to practice mindfulness meditation, start by sitting in a comfortable chair or cushion. Place your hands in your lap. With your eyes open, take a few deep breaths, utilizing the breathing style discussed in previous chapters: in through your nose and out through your mouth.

After about a minute, close your eyes and focus your attention on your body. Focus on the weight of your body on the chair, the physical points of contact between you and your surroundings. Focus on the feeling of your back against the chair, your feet against the floor, and your hands against your lap. Leave your attention here for a few minutes.

Next, focus your attention on your breathing. Visualize the breath entering and exiting your body. Think about how each breath feels. Feel the sensation of your diaphragm inflating and deflating with each breath. Think about the speed at which your breath is escaping and whether your breath feels cool or warm.

If at any point you find yourself feeling angry, simply observe the emotion without judging it or engaging it. Examine your emotion and try to visualize it in your body. Where do you see your anger? Does it lie in your throat, or your stomach, or perhaps your shoulders? What color is it? Is it hot or cold? Does it move around or is it static? Take a few minutes to try to identify characteristics about your anger with the intent of getting to know it. Then, refocus your attention on your breathing. Continue meditating for a few moments before gently opening your eyes and registering how you're feeling. It's okay if you still feel angry. Simply acknowledge the emotion and accept it. If you are feeling differently to when you began your meditation, take note of the change in your feelings.

There are other methods of meditation and I encourage you to experiment with different techniques in order to find one that suits you. It may take some time for you to get the hang of it and you may feel a little silly trying it, but if you persist with it, it is only a matter of time before you start seeing positive results.

Chapter 8:
Change Your Way of Thinking

Anger can be a powerful motivator and can lead to great things if you can remain in control of it and utilize it to take assertive action toward positive outcomes that are not harmful to others. However, anger is a passionate emotion and can be a difficult beast to tame. If left untamed, it can control the way that you think. If you are unprepared for your anger, it can easily get the better of you and drive you toward actions that may be detrimental to your well-being and the well-being of others.

You must always remember that *you* are in control of your actions, not your anger. While you can't control the turbulence of life, nor can you control the way that you feel about certain situations, there are some things that you do have control over. You can control your awareness of your own anger and the effect it has on the people around you. You can control the way that you react to your anger. You can control how you communicate your anger. With practice, you can even control the way that you think about situations that may lead to anger.

COGNITIVE RESTRUCTURING

There is a correlation between thought and emotion. The two processes occur in the brain and are closely linked to each other. One affects the other. A certain thought can spark an emotion in you, or indeed several emotions. The thought of approaching retirement may make you feel excited at the prospect of having more free time but it may also make you feel nostalgic for years gone by and nervous about entering the next phase of your life. At the same time, different emotions can cause different thoughts to go through your mind. The excitement you feel about getting more free time may lead you to thinking about what you can do with that free time. The feeling of nostalgia may make you recall all the good times you've had with your coworkers and company. The feeling of nervousness may make you think uncertain thoughts, such as whether your finances can sustain retirement or whether you are emotionally ready to retire.

Just as anger can lead to angry thoughts, angry thoughts can lead to anger. Often, people who have a problem with anger don't even notice their angry thoughts. Angry thoughts become an automatic way of thinking. Angry thoughts lead to anger, which in turn leads to more angry thoughts. It creates a cycle of anger that will make you feel worse and worse as recurring angry thoughts flash into your mind over and over.

It is possible to break this cycle by taking a close look at your angry thoughts and analyzing a situation more objectively to see if you are interpreting it correctly. People who are angry are more prone to taking things personally and seeking conflict that may not actually be there. Have you ever had an angry conversation with someone in a public place and spotted some of the people around you looking your way?

You might see them looking and think to yourself, "Why are they staring at me?" or, "These people should mind their own business" or, "They're staring at me because they think I'm a jerk." However, how accurate are these thoughts? When thinking about the situation from an objective viewpoint, rather than from a place of anger, it's probably more likely that those people were simply glancing over in response to the raised volume of your voice. They probably couldn't care less about your conversation and went straight back to their day once they saw what the source of the sound was.

When you are angry, you come to automatically expect negativity from other people and you tend to see hostility where there is none to be found. In order to manage your anger, it is important to recognize and challenge these thoughts.

In the mid-1950s, psychologist Albert Ellis developed a technique called cognitive restructuring. This technique can be used to control and change negative thoughts by reframing the situation that has triggered them. Since its development, cognitive restructuring has been used successfully to treat a wide variety of conditions, including depression, post-traumatic stress disorder, anxiety, social phobias, relationship issues, addictions, and stress.

In this chapter, we will teach you how to use cognitive restructuring to analyze and reframe your angry thoughts. With practice, this is a technique that you will be able to use regularly, not just to address angry thoughts, but all types of negative thoughts.

CALM YOURSELF

If you are still feeling angry from the situation you have experienced, you are going to have a hard time effectively utilizing cognitive restructuring. Therefore, the first step in the process is to calm yourself. Practice the relaxation techniques that were discussed in the previous chapters of this book, techniques such as deep breathing or muscle relaxation. Go to your calm-down kit if you need to. In fact, you can keep your calm-down kit next to the notepad you use for cognitive reframing.

Once you have successfully calmed yourself and reached a state of mind where you can be rational and objective, proceed to the next step.

IDENTIFY THE SITUATION

Think about the situation that made you angry. For now, just think about it in terms of cold, hard facts. Describe for yourself the event or series of events as they happened.

In order to clearly outline the process of cognitive restructuring, let's refer to the example below.

"The person I was seeing romantically broke up with me via text message."

This clearly defines the situation that has caused your anger in basic terms, without talking about emotion just yet.

ANALYZE YOUR MOOD

Next, write down the emotions you felt during this situation. Try to get down the entire range of emotions you felt, not just anger. Be sure to stick to just the emotions felt, not the thoughts associated with these emotions. For example, "I deserved more than just a text message," would be a thought, whereas the emotions associated with the thought would be anger, frustration, insecurity, and humiliation.

Once you have identified all the emotions you felt, write down what specifically about the situation made you angry. Was it the fact that the person broke up with you? Was it the fact that they didn't take the time to meet with you in person? Was it both? Whatever it was that made you angry, write it down. Even if the reason for your anger seems petty when you're looking at it on paper, be honest with yourself and leave nothing out.

IDENTIFY YOUR AUTOMATIC THOUGHTS

Next, identify and write down the thoughts that automatically went through your mind immediately after the event. These thoughts will most likely be negative and will be based upon your negative views of yourself and the world around you. If you are an angry person, your automatic thoughts will be motivated by emotions associated with anger, specific to the type of anger you exhibit. For example, if you are prone to a self-abusive style of anger, your automatic thoughts will be self-abusive in nature.

Typical types of automatic response include:

- Self-evaluated thoughts ie. "I'm not worth a face-to-face breakup."
- Thoughts about the evaluation of others ie. "They were always too good for me."
- Evaluative thoughts about other people ie. "They must be seeing someone else."
- Thoughts about coping strategies ie. "I really need a drink."
- Thoughts of avoidance ie. "I just want to be alone."

You may have more automatic thoughts than this so examine your thoughts carefully to make sure that you haven't missed any.

FIND OBJECTIVE SUPPORTIVE EVIDENCE

Now that you have written down the automatic thoughts that went through your mind when you experienced the triggering situation, identify and write down evidence that objectively supports your automatic thoughts. The goal of cognitive restructuring is to be honest with yourself and look at the situation from both sides. This means acknowledging your angry thoughts and trying to see if they are justifiable.

Here are some examples of supportive evidence for the previous automatic thoughts:

- "We hadn't been seeing each other for very long."
- "They were a very accomplished and attractive person."
- "We had been spending less and less time together lately."

FIND OBJECTIVE CONTRADICTORY EVIDENCE

Next, examine your automatic thoughts from the other side of the scale. Identify and write down evidence that is contradictory to your automatic thoughts.

Here are some examples of contradictory evidence:

- "The time that we spent together had been enjoyable."
- "I am an accomplished person with many friends that care about me."
- "My partner was always honest in their interactions with me."
- "We had a lot in common."

Here, we can see that these statements tend to be fairer and more rational than the automatic thoughts. They are less focused on negativity and generally consider the situation on a wider scale, taking an open view as opposed to the narrow view that comes from looking at things from a place of negativity.

IDENTIFY FAIR AND BALANCED THOUGHTS

Now that you've looked at both sides of the situation, you are better equipped to take a fair and balanced view of the situation. Consider both the supportive evidence and the contradictory evidence and decide which evidence is more valid. It's possible that you may combine two pieces of information together to form statements that are more accurate than either individual side. Write down these statements, read them back to yourself, and really think hard about each statement. Decide whether each statement is balanced and rewrite them if you need to. If you are unsure as to whether you are managing a successful balance, try discussing the situation with your friends to see what they think.

Once you have arrived at a balanced view, right down your balanced thoughts. For example:

- "While our relationship was enjoyable at times, our recent interactions had not been as fun."
- "We are both interesting people, but our personalities didn't match."
- "The way they ended the relationship was inappropriate, but also out of character. It might have been a result of things going on in their life that I don't know about."

MONITOR YOUR PRESENT MOOD

Now that you have a clearer view of the situation, write down how you are feeling now. It is likely that your feelings toward the situation will have improved from before you started this exercise and you are feeling less angry. The time taken to reevaluate the situation, as well as the process itself, both act in delaying your anger, refocusing your mind, and presenting a more objective perspective on the events of the situation.

Now that you are in a calmer state, think about what you should do next. It's possible that after looking objectively at the situation, you have decided to pursue no further action. You may decide that the breakup was for the best and that the person probably had a good reason for ending it with a text. You may decide to move on and leave the door open in case they wish to communicate with you more effectively in the future.

If you do wish to take further action, you will be in a better state of mind to think of a course of action that is going to lead to a positive outcome. Rather than calling them up and leaving a tirade of angry voicemail messages, you choose to send them a polite text that tells them that you understand but feel hurt by the way they ended it. You may ask them if it would be okay to meet in person so that you can discuss the matter further.

However you choose to respond to the situation, by performing cognitive restructuring you can guarantee that the action you choose to take will be rational and well-thought out, rather than an automatic, potentially destructive, response.

Chapter 9:
You Are Not Alone

A nger is something that everyone deals with. It is therefore something that everyone is familiar with. You may feel alienated by the intense rage that you have to deal with. You may feel like a monster because of the thoughts and feelings that go through your mind on a daily basis. However, this is far from the truth.

The truth is that the world is an angry place and it only seems to be getting angrier. According to a 2019 NPR-IBM Watson Health poll, 84% of surveyed people said that Americans are angrier now than they were a generation ago. When asked about their own feelings, 42% of those surveyed said that they were angrier now than they were last year. According to a separate survey, "the overall prevalence of inappropriate, intense, or poorly controlled anger in the U.S. population was 7.8%" (Okuda et al., 2014). Anger is an emotion that many people have difficulty controlling. Even though you might sometimes feel alienated because of your anger, it's important to know that you are definitely not alone.

There is always someone to talk to when you are feeling angry. Everybody can relate to feelings of anger and can sympathize with actions done in anger. No matter how heinous you think your actions are or how ashamed you are at having done them, it is important not to keep your feelings to yourself. Don't sweep your feelings and actions under the rug. Own them. Confront them. Deal with them. If you can't do it alone, do it with some help from the world around you.

FRIENDS

Friendships are among the most valuable relationships we have. There are some things that you can talk about with your friends that you just can't with family members. Friends can keep us grounded and provide a voice of reason that we are more inclined to listen to than people we are related to. We often seek help from our friends and they seek help from us sometimes. This back-and-forth of cooperation helps create strong bonds. Friends accept us for who we are and make us feel more confident to face whatever life throws at us.

Despite knowing all this, you might feel hesitant to talk to your friends about your anger. If you see your anger as a problem or a personal flaw, you might be ashamed of admitting to it. You might fear losing the respect of your friends or you might feel that you don't want to burden them with your problems.

You don't have to talk to your friends about your anger if you don't want to. You certainly shouldn't feel the need to tell everyone you know about your problems. No matter how close with someone you are, you may not feel comfortable talking with them about your anger. That's perfectly fine. Seek out someone else you can talk with; perhaps someone whose opinion of you is less important to you than those of your close friends, for example, a therapist.

If you are unsure whether or not to broach the subject of your anger with your friends, it might be helpful to write down the pros and cons of doing so. You might find that the benefits of talking to your friends about your anger greatly outweigh the risks.

Talking to your friends about your anger may be difficult, but it can also be very important, not just for your mental health but also for maintaining your relationships. If you are an angry person, it's likely that your friends have noticed. Choosing to talk to them about your anger lets them know that you acknowledge that you have anger issues and that you're trying to address them. If they were not already aware of your anger, talking to them about it would allow them to understand your feelings and actions better, helping explain why you may behave a certain way.

If you're going to try to talk to your friends about your anger, it's best to choose a friend you trust as the first person you talk to. This will make it easier for you to gauge their reaction to what you're saying and hone your approach if you wish to discuss it with other people. Choosing a setting where you both will feel comfortable, whether it be public or private, quiet or noisy, indoors or outdoors. It's important to try to make your friend feel comfortable as well, as their reaction may dictate whether or not you feel you have accomplished successful communication by the end of it.

It's important to note that different people will display different reactions to news regarding mental health issues like anger. Some people will react dramatically to the news. Others may feel awkward and not know how to respond. They may even say that you're totally fine and there's no problem with how you express your anger. When you're gauging your friend's response, remember to think about their own personality and what you know about them. They may respond dramatically because they have never encountered someone with anger management issues before. They may not know how to respond because they relate very closely to how you feel.

However they react, you have succeeded in opening the door to communication. Being able to talk to someone about your anger, particularly someone that you get along well with, will relieve a huge amount of tension from both yourself and your relationship with this person. You may even find that your friend opens up to you about issues they are having. If this happens, remember to be supportive of them—their problems are just as important as your own. Listen to them, tell them that you are still their friend, and help them in any way that you can. By developing a dialogue about your feelings, you will come to better understand each other and your friendship will become stronger because of it.

GROUP THERAPY

If you are worried about the prospect of discussing your anger issues with your friends for fear of losing them, there are many support groups available that provide an intimate, yet detached platform for you to talk about your feelings. Group therapy not only allows you to tell others how you feel but it also gives you the opportunity to gain insights into how other people feel and how they react to similar situations. By listening to the stories of others, you can relate to them and gain a better understanding of your own anger.

Group therapy involves one or more therapists working with several people at a time and is available in a wide variety of locations, from private hospitals to local community centers. As outlined by VeryWell Mind, the goals and principles of group therapy involve:

- Instilling hope by involving people at varying stages of the healing process. By seeing people who have been in the group for a while and are making progress, newcomers to the group can be hopeful that it might work for them.

- Showing people suffering from anger management issues that they are not alone and that many people are also struggling with the same issues.
- Allowing group members to help each other, learning from each other's journeys.
- Providing a safe and supportive environment that allows group members to develop their social skills and experiment with new forms of communication.
- Allowing group members to observe and model the behavior of members that are making progress.
- Sharing feelings and experiences to help relieve the stress, guilt, and pain caused from holding them inside.
- Instilling a sense of responsibility in group members and making them realize that they are responsible for their thoughts and actions.

There are several types of therapy groups, each with their own procedures and tones. In general, they can be broken down into two broad groups, psychoeducational and process-oriented. Psychoeducational groups follow a more educational structure and seek to provide members with the information they need to cope with anger. Process-oriented groups are more focused on sharing experiences and forging bonds and connections between members.

These two broad groups can be further broken down by varying discussion topics and structures.

Self-help groups are generally led by someone who may not be a health professional but has struggled with and overcome issues to do with anger in their lives. Medication groups focus on ensuring that all members are aware of the correct usage of any medication they are prescribed to take.

Interpersonal therapy groups focus on the members' current relationships and problems. Encounter groups are more immersive and try to provoke greater change in members by introducing them to potentially uncomfortable situations. Groups that use psychodrama allow group members to act out specific portions of their lives to provoke strong emotions. These reenactments are followed up with group analysis and discussion.

The number of participants, duration, and frequency of group therapy ranges between the different styles. It is advised that you do your research before attempting group therapy but don't be too hesitant. All group therapy platforms offer a safe and judgment-free environment, so you have nothing to lose by giving them a go. Similarly, don't be too quick to give up on group therapy. It may take you more than one visit to gather the courage to speak; longer still to notice any visible progress. Commit to the therapy. An essential rule of almost any group is that it is vital that all members attend every session, arrive on time, and stay for the entire session. This rule is in place not just for your benefit, but for the benefit of the entire group. If you miss a session, not only will you miss valuable information and potential breakthroughs, but you will disrupt the progress of the entire group.

ONLINE FORUMS

You may be the type who feels too uncomfortable to share your feelings with your friends. You may even be so shy as to avoid sharing your anger with anyone face-to-face. If this applies to you, try turning to the internet for avenues to share your feelings. Mental health websites such as ReachOut.com provide online forums where you can express your anger and receive advice from trained mental health professionals. They provide a safe, supportive, and anonymous space for you to talk through your feelings. Websites such as these often contain a lot of useful information in the form of articles and discussions. You may find that taking part in an online discussion and reading about what other people are going through can help you tackle your own issues with anger management.

If you find that this is still too great a leap for you to take, consider starting your own personal blog. As mentioned in earlier chapters, writing down your feelings can succeed in regulating your anger by getting it out in a healthy expression. By reading what you have written, you will gain insights into your emotions. You may keep the blog private if you wish, but if you ever feel the desire to share the information with other people that may be going through similar problems, you can make the blog public. Using your past experiences to help other people can give you a sense of pride and give you confidence in your ability to deal with future problems.

PROFESSIONAL HELP

A nger is a well-researched topic and, as such, there are several options when it comes to anger therapy. There are many benefits to consulting with a professional therapist. They will be able to qualify and quantify your anger and bring to your attention any underlying diagnoses as well. Anger is tied to several mental health conditions such as depression, bipolarism, oppositional defiant behavior (ODD), narcissistic personality disorder, and post traumatic stress disorder (PTSD). It's possible that your anger is a symptom of any one of these disorders and you may not be aware of it. A therapist can also help if your anger has caused you to fall into patterns of dangerous behavior, such as substance abuse or physical abuse.

A therapist can teach you necessary skills to manage your emotions and can address the underlying emotions and memories that have the potential to be the root of your anger.

Although you may associate seeking professional help with "crazy people," it is common for people, even those considered to be of sound mental health, to talk to professional therapists. In fact, people who are mentally healthy often attribute their mental health to regular therapy sessions.

When it comes to anger, it is advisable that you seek professional help if you are:

- in trouble with the law as a result of anger issues
- lashing out physically at people
- threatening violence toward other people
- experiencing constant, uncontrollable arguments
- losing control of yourself when you are angry

- resorting to self-harm as a means for coping with anger (this includes substance abuse)

Professional anger management treatment can come in inpatient and outpatient varieties.

A residential or inpatient anger management treatment center will allow you to reside in accommodations that are not only serene but also give you quick access to mental health professionals. Being in a comfortable, supportive, and serene environment will have a positive effect on your mood and provide a much-needed separation or distance between yourself and situations in the outside world that may cause you stress. Having close access to dedicated treatment staff in a controlled environment will allow you to quickly learn techniques to manage your anger.

If you are unable to commit to a residential treatment program, there are many outpatient options of therapy that will provide intense individual counselling to help you manage your anger. Counselling often consists of six to eight weeks of weekly visits with a therapist who will talk you through your anger and prepare you for limited follow-up care moving forward.

Whichever treatment option you decide to go with, make sure to do your research. Look for treatment centers that offer comprehensive assessment, treatment, and follow-up programs. Speak with the health professionals directly and ask them questions regarding their qualifications, methodology, and expected results. Compare the costs of various programs and check to see if your health insurance will cover it.

In order to get the most out of seeing a therapist, make sure that you take a collaborative approach with your therapist.

Try not to see them as someone who is going to fix you. Instead, think of them as a teammate who is going to help you help yourself. Make sure to be honest with both them and yourself. There is no point spending good money on a therapist only for them to misdiagnose you because you withhold information. Remember that results can take time to achieve and it is important to remain vigilant and consistent with your treatment routine. Put the appointment in your calendar and stick with it. Think of going to therapy as another form of self-maintenance, like having a shower or brushing your teeth. Most of all, be sure to communicate well and often with your therapist, even if it is difficult. The times that it is difficult are the times when therapy is most important, so be sure to have your therapist's number on hand when the going gets tough.

Conclusion

"Anger is my meat; I sup upon myself and so shall starve with feeding." The line from William Shakespeare's Coriolanus can serve as a reminder that anger, as satisfying as it may be to act upon or hold onto, will eventually destroy us from the inside if it is all that we know.

We all experience anger at some point in our lives and we are rarely given the opportunity to learn skills to cope with the emotion. If you grew up like I did, you went to school and attended classes for mathematics, information technology, physical education, music, art, and science; all valuable topics that would develop our minds and open them up to new ideas and avenues of thought. Yet there were no classes that actively sought to increase our emotional intelligence. Growing up, there were no classes for empathy, meditation, or cognitive restructuring. It was assumed that growing up in a social environment would automatically give us the tools to process emotions in a healthy way. By observing our peers, our teachers, and our family members, we would have everything we need to learn how to effectively process emotions like anger, without the need for additional classes on the subject.

However, when anger is so rampant in our society, how was social interaction ever going to be an effective method of developing emotional intelligence? Everybody experiences anger in a different way and therefore has to overcome different obstacles when processing their anger. Some people display open and aggressive anger, while others repress their anger and hold onto it inwardly. Everybody has their own method of dealing with anger and very few people can actually consistently process their anger in a healthy way. Trying to learn how to manage anger from studying the people around you is like trying to learn how to play basketball by watching the amateur and professional leagues of every sport that involves a ball. Yes, these sports have a common element, but they are entirely different games played by players of varying levels of skill. You may pick up a useful technique here and there, but mostly you're going to end up confused and not great at basketball.

Emotional intelligence is a very important part of life and it deserves to be developed further. These days, it is widely accepted as an important part of childhood education and this has seen a change in the way education is handled in many countries. More and more, we are seeing early learning programs that use breathing techniques and positive visualization to promote alpha waves in students' minds and teach children how to connect with their emotions in a constructive way.

However, just because you may have missed out on these opportunities as a child, as I did, doesn't mean that you can't make them a part of your life now. It's never too late to develop your emotional intelligence and learn how to master your emotions. In fact, there are some benefits to studying the subject as an adult. When you're a child, learning is very much instinctual. A child's mind absorbs information and stores it away without having to understand the benefits of having the information. They will accept the information given to them as a rule, but lack the life experience to contextualize the information.

For example, at an early age, children will learn that it is not good to wish harm on someone out of anger. They may learn this from listening to or reading a story with a similar moral. Aesop's fable, the Bee and Jupiter, tells the story of a bee who ascended Mount Olympus to present an offering of honey from her hive to Jupiter, the king of the gods. Jupiter was delighted with the offering and promised to give the bee whatever she asked for in return. The bee asked Jupiter to give her a stinger, so that if any mortal dared to approach her honey, she could attack them. Jupiter was displeased with the request because he loved the race of man, but he could not refuse the bee's request because of his promise. So Jupiter told the bee that he would give her a stinger as promised, but warned her that using the stinger would come at the cost of her own life.

The moral of this story is that spiteful prayers are no better than curses in disguise. Upon hearing this story, a child will accept the lesson and understand that they shouldn't wish harm on someone, no matter the reason. Children can understand this lesson on a conceptual level, but they themselves have probably not yet experienced or been presented with this kind of situation in the real world. An adult, on the other hand, will have lived long enough to have felt the sting of someone else's attack. They will have no doubt been put in a situation where they felt hatred for someone that was so strong that they wished them harm. They are better equipped to understand the implications of the story at a real world level and understand the consequences of spiteful wishes and actions by remembering past experiences.

Adults have the benefit of a lifetime of experiences of which they can draw upon when trying to learn how to manage their emotions. They are better equipped to understand the real world consequences of their actions and the importance of self-improvement in this capacity. They also have the benefit of being better equipped to understand the science behind emotions and thought processes, meaning they can approach their issues at an intellectual level, rather than an instinctive level.

The important lesson to take away from this is that it is never too late to improve yourself. In many ways, you are more equipped to deal with your anger now than you would have been as a child. You have already taken the hardest step in accepting that your anger is an issue that needs addressing. By choosing to read this book to the end, you have not only chosen to accept your anger but you have accepted that while you may not be able to rid yourself of the emotion itself, you can control the way in which you act on it.

Throughout this book, we have given you the tools to come to a better understanding of your anger and how it works. We have highlighted the importance of understanding your anger, coming to terms with it, and understanding the effect it has on the people around you. You have been equipped with a variety of tools with which to deal with your anger; how to deal with flare ups and how to live with your anger on a daily basis. You have been given advice on communication so that you can protect your relationships from damage that your anger may cause. Hopefully, you have been given a different perspective with which to look at situations that may cause you anger. You have taken several positive steps toward dealing with your anger, enriching your mind and becoming aware that the problem is not only solvable, but that there are many avenues available for you to explore in order to solve it.

The next steps are up to you. I would advise taking a day or two to process all of this information. Really examine your anger in terms of the six dimensions of anger and your typical expressions of anger. Think about which anger management strategies talked about in this book would be most effective for your anger type. Do you tend to express your anger physically? In this case, picking up a physical activity may be the best way to release your pent up aggression. Do you tend to be more passive-aggressive? In this case, becoming better at writing down your feelings will prevent you from holding anger within or lashing out in sarcastic mockery. Look at your anger from a scientific standpoint and objectively decide which avenue to take.

Next, I would take some time to examine your lifestyle and think of the practicality of the anger management strategies. Perhaps you don't have the time to go for an hour walk everyday to clear your mind. That's okay. The same effect can be gained from a five minute heavy-bag session. Not enough space in your house for a punching bag? No problem. Load up your iPod with music that not only explores the anger felt by the artists composing them but also music that is proven to make you feel calm. Listen to that on the way to work. Come up with a plan to incorporate ongoing anger management strategies into your routine. Don't try to change too much of your life at once, as this will make it difficult to stick with the anger management strategies you've introduced. Implement one strategy, see how it goes, get used to doing it regularly. Once it has successfully become an integrated part of your routine, pick your next strategy and introduce it into your life.

Understand that emotional stability is an ongoing process. Self-maintenance is work, and just like any work, it will be hard at times. However, it is important to stick with it because the rewards are worth the effort. If you succeed in implementing strategies to manage your anger that work for you, the positive results you see will make you feel better overall. Being armed with the ability to recognize when you are getting angry and having a plan to control the anger will give you peace of mind and allow you to worry less about when your next outburst may happen. Every time you succeed in processing your anger healthily, congratulate yourself. See your confidence in your control over your emotions increase with every success, paving the road to true mastery of your inner world.

Once you are confident in your ability to control your anger, I recommend reaching out to the people around you. Apologize to the people you feel you may have wronged or alienated with your anger. Explain to them that you are working on controlling your behavior and truly feel that you are a different person. They may not be ready to forgive you just yet, but give them time. Whether or not they forgive you, it is important to connect with them and leave the door open for the reparation of trust.

I hope this book has been a helpful resource in your quest for managing your anger. I wish you all the best in your journey and hope that you find the peace that you are looking for. If this book has helped you and you know someone else who may benefit from its contents, please pass on its teachings. The world is far from perfect but the better everyone is at understanding their emotions and dealing with them in a healthy way, the better the place the world can be.

References

8 ways to deal with anger. (2019). Reachout.Com.
https://au.reachout.com/articles/8-ways-to-deal-with-anger

Abdelgaffar, M. (n.d.). Toddler with red Adidas sweatshirt. In
pexels.com. https://www.pexels.com/photo/toddler-with-red-adidas-sweat-shirt-783941/

Ackerman, C. (2017, July 26). *Your ultimate guide on group therapy
(+activities & topic ideas).* PositivePsychology.Com.

https://positivepsychology.com/group-therapy/

Aesop, Paul, A., & Artist Book Works. (1993). *The Bee and Jupiter :
from Aesop's fables.* A.P. Kennedy, Jr.

Akers, M., & Porter, G. (2018, October 8). *What is emotional
intelligence (EQ)?* Psych Central. https://psychcentral.com/lib/what-is-emotional-intelligence-eq/

al'Absi, M., Carr, S. B., & Bongard, S. (2007). Anger and
psychobiological changes during smoking abstinence and in response
to acute stress: Prediction of smoking relapse. *International Journal
of Psychophysiology : Official Journal of the International
Organization of Psychophysiology, 66*(2), 109–115.
https://doi.org/10.1016/j.ijpsycho.2007.03.016

Andrews, M. (2017, February 17). *10 types of anger: What's your
anger style?* Life Supports.
https://lifesupportscounselling.com.au/types-of-anger-styles-of-anger/

Anger. (2019, November 21). Good Therapy.
https://www.goodtherapy.org/learn-about-therapy/issues/anger#:~:text=If%20you%20or%20a%20loved

Anger management: 10 tips to tame your temper. (2020, February
29). Mayo Clinic. https://www.mayoclinic.org/healthy-lifestyle/adult-health/in-depth/anger-management/art-20045434

Anger management therapy - Type of therapy. (n.d.).
Careersinpsychology.Org. Retrieved August 25, 2020, from
https://careersinpsychology.org/anger-management-
therapy/#:~:text=Group%20therapy%20provides%20an%20opportu
nity

Anger statistics. (n.d.). The British Association of Anger Management.
https://www.angermanage.co.uk/anger-statistics/

Assertive communication: An anger management technique. (n.d.).
Impact Factory. Retrieved August 25, 2020, from
https://www.impactfactory.com/library/assertive-communication-
anger-management-technique

Bariso, J. (2015, November 23). *How emotionally intelligent people
deal with anger.* Inc.Com. https://www.inc.com/justin-bariso/how-
emotionally-intelligent-people-deal-with-
anger.html#:~:text=Anger%20can%20be%20good%2D%2Dif%20kept
%20under%20control.&text=Anger%20is%20an%20extremely%20po
werful%20emotion.&text=Emotional%20intelligence%20(EQ)%2C%2
0or

Bertone, H. J. (2017, June 9). *Which type of meditation is right for
me?* Healthline; Healthline Media.
https://www.healthline.com/health/mental-health/types-of-
meditation#mindfulness-meditation

Chamorro-Premuzic, T. (2013, May 29). *Can you really improve your
emotional intelligence?* Harvard Business Review.
https://hbr.org/2013/05/can-you-really-improve-your-em

Cherry, K. (2009, November 24). *An overview of group therapy.*
Verywell Mind; Verywellmind. https://www.verywellmind.com/what-
is-group-therapy-2795760

Cherry, K. (2020, May 17). *The purpose of emotions.* Verywell Mind;
Verywellmind. https://www.verywellmind.com/the-purpose-of-
emotions-2795181

Cognitive restructuring: Reducing stress by changing your thinking.
(2014). Mindtools.
https://www.mindtools.com/pages/article/newtcs_81.htm

Controlling anger before it controls you. (n.d.). *American Psychological Association*. https://www.apa.org/topics/anger/control

Cuncic, A. (2020, August 3). *How to practice progressive muscle relaxation: A step-by-step plan to relax your body*. Verywell Mind. https://www.verywellmind.com/how-do-i-practice-progressive-muscle-relaxation-3024400

Dewitt, S. (2020, May 19). *Managing anger with healthy habits*. Betterhelp. https://www.betterhelp.com/advice/anger/managing-anger-with-healthy-habits/

Evans, S. (2014, March 16). *People really do see red when they're angry and it's all because our ancestors linked it with danger*. Mail Online. https://www.dailymail.co.uk/news/article-2581997/People-really-red-theyre-angry-ancestors-linked-danger.html

Fernandez, E. (2016). *The angry personality: A representation on six dimensions of anger expression*.

Friendship and mental health. (2018, August 14). Mental Health Foundation. https://www.mentalhealth.org.uk/a-to-z/f/friendship-and-mental-health

Hensley, S. (2019, June 26). *Poll: Americans say we're angrier than a generation ago*. NPR.Org. https://www.npr.org/sections/health-shots/2019/06/26/735757156/poll-americans-say-were-angrier-than-a-generation-ago#:~:text=Some%2084%25%20of%20people%20surveyed

Holland, K. (2019, January 29). *How to control anger: 25 tips to manage your anger and feel calmer*. Healthline. https://www.healthline.com/health/mental-health/how-to-control-anger#6

j.mt_photography. (n.d.). Man walking on rocky terrain. In *pexels.com*. https://www.pexels.com/photo/man-walking-on-rocky-terrain-3680119/

Karmin, A. (2016, August 4). *How to change angry thoughts*. Psych Central. https://blogs.psychcentral.com/anger/2016/08/how-to-change-angry-thoughts/

Kim, C. (n.d.). Volcano erupting at night under a starry sky. In *pexels.com*. https://www.pexels.com/photo/volcano-erupting-at-night-under-starry-sky-4220967/

meo. (n.d.-a). Photo of head bust. In *pexels.com*. https://www.pexels.com/photo/photo-of-head-bust-print-artwork-724994/

mikoto.raw. (n.d.-b). Photo of woman using mobile phone. In *pexels.com*. https://www.pexels.com/photo/photo-of-woman-using-mobile-phone-3367850/

Millennial, B. (n.d.). Selective focus photo of man using laptop. In *pexels.com*. https://www.pexels.com/photo/selective-focus-photo-of-man-using-laptop-1438081/

Mills, H. (n.d.). *Psychology of anger: Emotional intelligence.* PermiaCare. Retrieved August 25, 2020, from https://www.pbmhmr.com/poc/view_doc.php?type=doc&id=16135&cn=474

Morin, A. (2020, August 3). *11 anger management strategies to help you calm down.* Verywell Mind. https://www.verywellmind.com/anger-management-strategies-4178870

Okuda, M., Picazo, J., Olfson, M., Hasin, D. S., Liu, S.-M., Bernardi, S., & Blanco, C. (2014). Prevalence and correlates of anger in the community: Results from a national survey. *CNS Spectrums, 20*(02), 130–139. https://doi.org/10.1017/s1092852914000182

Pixabay. (n.d.). Red stop sign. In *pexels.com*. https://www.pexels.com/photo/red-stop-sign-39080/

Saghir, Z., Syeda, J. N., Muhammad, A. S., & Balla Abdalla, T. H. (2018). The amygdala, sleep debt, sleep deprivation, and the emotion of anger: A possible connection? *Cureus.* https://doi.org/10.7759/cureus.2912

Santos-Longhurst, A. (2019, February 4). *Do I have anger issues? How to identify and treat an angry outlook.* Healthline; Healthline Media. https://www.healthline.com/health/anger-issues#symptoms

Scott, E. (2020a, January 31). *How to manage anger and stress.* Verywell Mind. https://www.verywellmind.com/the-effects-of-anger-and-stress-3145076

Scott, E. (2020b, July 1). *How to reduce stress with breathing exercises.* Verywell Mind. https://www.verywellmind.com/how-to-reduce-stress-with-breathing-exercises-3144508

Seltzer, L. (2008, July 11). *What your anger may be hiding: Reflections on the most seductive - and addictive - of human emotions.* Psychology Today. https://www.psychologytoday.com/au/blog/evolution-the-self/200807/what-your-anger-may-be-hiding

Shakespeare, W., Parker, R. B., & Folio Society (London, England. (2008). *Coriolanus.* Folio Society.

Smith, J.-M. (n.d.). Person holding fountain pen. In *pexels.com.* https://www.pexels.com/photo/person-holding-fountain-pen-211291/

Stahl, A. (2018, May 29). *5 ways to develop your emotional intelligence.* Forbes. https://www.forbes.com/sites/ashleystahl/2018/05/29/5-ways-to-develop-your-emotional-intelligence/#2c70b9316976

Stavrinos, S. (n.d.). Monochrome photography of people shaking hands. In *pexels.com.* https://www.pexels.com/photo/monochrome-photography-of-people-shaking-hands-814544/

Strategies for controlling your anger: Keeping anger in check. (2011). *American Psychological Association.* https://www.apa.org/topics/strategies-controlling-anger

The effects of emotions on communication. (n.d.). Universal Class. Retrieved August 25, 2020, from https://www.universalclass.com/articles/business/communication-studies/the-effects-of-emotions-on-communications.htm

Thorpe, M. (2017, July 5). *12 science-based benefits of meditation.* Healthline; Healthline Media. https://www.healthline.com/nutrition/12-benefits-of-meditation#section10

Treating anger disorders: Anger management treatment program options. (2019). PsychGuides. https://www.psychguides.com/anger-management/treatment/

Ulinwa, J. (n.d.). Photo of woman wearing red boxing gloves. In *pexels.com.* https://www.pexels.com/photo/photo-of-woman-wearing-red-boxing-gloves-3225889/

Umoh, R. (2018, August 8). *These 5 simple body language tricks can help you build trust with anyone.* CNBC. https://www.cnbc.com/2018/08/07/5-simple-body-language-tricks-to-build-trust-with-anyone.html

Understanding anger and anger management strategies. (2018). MensLine Australia. https://mensline.org.au/how-to-deal-with-anger/understanding-anger-and-anger-management-strategies/

Zetlin, M. (2020, February 7). *How to calm your own anger in 60 seconds or less, according to a psychologist.* Inc.Com. https://www.inc.com/minda-zetlin/managing-anger-emotional-intelligence-calming.html

Zhaoyang, R., Sliwinski, M. J., Martire, L. M., & Smyth, J. M. (2018). Age differences in adults' daily social interactions: An ecological momentary assessment study. *Psychology and Aging, 33*(4), 607–618. https://doi.org/10.1037/pag0000242

Made in the USA
Columbia, SC
20 November 2020